CASES *for* MARKETING MANAGEMENT

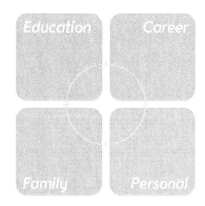

Taken from:

Prentice Hall Custom Business Resources

Custom Publishing

New York   Boston   San Francisco
London   Toronto   Sydney   Tokyo   Singapore   Madrid
Mexico City   Munich   Paris   Cape Town   Hong Kong   Montreal

Director of Database Publishing: Michael Payne
Senior Sponsoring Editor: Robin J. Lazrus
Development Editor: Catherine O'Keefe
Marketing Manager: Amy Dawson
Assistant Editor: Ana Díaz-Caneja
Operations Manager: Eric M. Kenney
Production Product Manager: Jennifer Berry
Cover Designer: Renée Sartell

Cover Art: Courtesy of EyeWire/Getty Images and PhotoDisc/Getty Images. Photodisc, "Globe surrounded by business people on computer monitors," courtesy of Photodisc/Getty Images. Dave Cutler (Artist), "Man Dropping Coins Into Glass Jar," courtesy of David Cutler/Images.com. Dave Cutler (Artist), "Three Coins in Glass Jar," courtesy of David Cutler/Images.com.

This special edition published in cooperation with Pearson Custom Publishing.

Printed in the United States of America.

Please visit our web site at *www.pearsoncustom.com*

Attention bookstores: For permission to return unused stock, call 800-777-6872.

ISBN–13: 9780536762573

ISBN–10: 0536762570

Package ISBN–13: N/A

Package ISBN–10: N/A

PEARSON CUSTOM PUBLISHING
501 Boylston Street, Suite 900
Boston, MA 02116

Editorial Advisory Board

Contents

Euro Disney: The First 100 Days

This is the most wonderful project we have ever done.

Michael Eisner, CEO,
The Walt Disney Company[1]

A horror made of cardboard, plastic, and appalling colors; a construction of hardened chewing gum and idiotic folklore taken straight out of comic books written for obese Americans.

Jean Cau, French Critic[2]

April 12, 1992 was a cool and hazy day in Marne-la-Vallee, France, home of the Euro Disney Resort complex. Built on a site one-fifth the size of Paris and 20 miles to its west, boasting scores of rides, attractions, hotels, restaurants, entertainment facilities, a campground, and even a championship golf course, Euro Disney opened that day on time and within its $4.4 billion budget.[3]

Roy Disney, nephew of the founder of The Walt Disney Company, addressed the opening day crowd from a platform half way up *Le Chateau De La Belle Au Bois Dormant* (The Sleeping Beauty Castle). He described the complex as an emotional homecoming for the family, which traced its roots to the French town of Isigny-sur-Mer. However, notwithstanding a $10 million ad campaign in anticipation of the opening, attendance at the event was less than some had expected. As evidence of a cool French reception to Euro Disney, commuter trains leading to the park were on strike, protesting staffing and security problems, residents of nearby villages demonstrated against the noise, and a terrorist bomb had just missed disabling nearby electrical facilities the night before.

Research Associate Robert Anthony prepared this case under the supervision of Professors Gary Loveman and Leonard Schlesinger as the basis for class discussion rather than to illustrate either effective or ineffective handling of an administrative situation. The case was prepared from published sources, and the Walt Disney Company is in no way responsible for the completeness, accuracy, or fairness of presentation of any information contained herein.

1

On June 9 Disney reported that attendance for the park's first seven weeks had been over 1.5 million.[4] While the company previously had projected 11 million in attendance for the first year, it was thought likely that the majority of visitors would be attracted before the wet and colder fall and winter seasons. Also, research showed that the attendance of nearby French residents, who were projected to account for half of the park's attendance, was running well below the expected rate.[5] In New York shares of The Walt Disney Company dropped 5% following the June attendance announcement.

On July 24 Euro Disney announced that revenues for its first quarter of operations were $489 million ($451 million at April 12 exchange rates), but that it would incur a loss for the fiscal year ending September 30, 1992. The company blamed the loss on the fact that it had geared up for a higher level of operations than had actually been attained. Attendance had been 3.6 million through July 22. Shares of Euro Disney, which traded on the French Bourse, dropped 2.75% following the announcement, capping a 31% drop since the opening of the park.[6]

Disney managers remained optimistic that Euro Disney would prove to be a dramatic extension of its founder's dream to "make people happy." Chairman Michael Eisner defended the performance of the park by stating that attendance at Euro Disney exceeded that of Disney's other three theme parks at comparable points in their history.[7] Euro Disney President Robert Fitzpatrick, who had predicted that Europe would become as important to the future success of the company as America,[8] stated that it was impossible to extrapolate meaningfully from the attendance figures at such an early point in the history of the complex.[9]

Still, after five years of controversy over whether various aspects of Disney's traditional approach would fit with French culture, prompting one critic to dub the project a "cultural Chernobyl,"[10] there seemed reason to wonder whether the magic of Disney's famous Magic Kingdom would be replicated in France.

Walt Disney Attractions

Disney Theme Parks

The Walt Disney Company, founded by Walt Disney and his brother Roy in 1923, consisted of theme parks and resort complexes, motion picture and television production and distribution, consumer products licensing, publishing and retail, and other limited entertainment ventures. **Exhibit 1** provides aggregate financial data for the Walt Disney Company and **Exhibit 2** provides segment data. Walt Disney Attractions consisted of theme parks, hotel and conference facilities, retail complexes, and other recreational properties. In 1991 71% of Walt Disney Attraction's revenues were derived from theme parks, 21% from hotels, and 8% from other sources.[11]

Disney's largest property was Walt Disney World Resort, located on 29,000 acres in Orlando, Florida and boasting three separate theme parks. The 98-acre Magic Kingdom theme park, opened in 1971, featured 45 attractions in seven themed lands and was the site's original park. The 110-acre Disney-MGM Studios Theme Park featured 13 attractions centered around Hollywood's movie industry, as well as contained a working film and television production facility. The EPCOT Center combined the educational Future World, which featured 14 educational and entertainment-oriented attractions in eight pavilions, with the culturally themed attractions of the World Showcase, consisting of six attractions in 11 "country pavilions."[12]

Disneyland, which opened in 1955, was the company's first theme park. Located near Los Angeles, California, it featured over 50 attractions in seven themed lands. Tokyo Disneyland was

2

designed by Disney but owned and operated by the Oriental Land Company. Its 114 acres was one and one-half times as large as the Disneyland in Southern California, but it was substantially similar in concept to this property.[13]

By early 1992, the company owned and operated hotel properties consisting of 17,000 rooms and 580,000 square feet of meeting space, through its development of its Florida property.[14] In 1990, over 50 million people visited Disney parks,[15] and 1991 attendance showed a slight decline due to economic recession (estimates for 1991 attendance ran as high as 57 million, including Tokyo Disneyland's 16 million).[16] In 1989, which was likely a typical year in recent experience, roughly twice as many people visited the larger Walt Disney World park than the Southern California Disneyland. In addition, it was estimated that 90% of theme park visitors were repeat customers,[17] and 5%, or well over two million people, flocked in from Europe annually.[18] The majority of Disney visitors were adults, many of whom were in their late twenties and had young children. In 1991 a day pass at Walt Disney World cost $34.75 and at Disneyland cost $27.50.[19] It was estimated that a typical family of four spent $30 per day, per person on meals, snacks, and souvenirs while on vacation at Walt Disney World.[20]

The core of Disney's success defied easy characterization. As one observer noted, "The difference that is Disney goes (very deep) into the American consciousness, for this is a company that sells myth and fantasy."[21]

In one sense, the Disney tradition of creative imagination drew its energy from the personality of Walt Disney himself. Walt was legendary within the company for his obsessive focus on creating products and experiences for his customers which epitomized "fun," and his life was an enthusiastic quest for new technologies, plans, and possibilities which would make this a reality. At the same time, the Disney magic had seemingly been institutionalized in a creative process and meticulous service delivery system which was able to consistently perpetuate a fantastic experience for each of millions of theme park visitors every year. Twenty six years after the death of its founder Disney still had as a primary objective "preserving the basic Disney values—quality, imagination, (and) guest service."[22]

At the center of the Disney theme park experience was the "theme." Disney parks were subdivided into a number of "lands," each of which revolved around a single motif in the nature of its rides and attractions, the costumes of employees, the architectural style of its buildings, and even the food and souvenirs sold within its boundaries. More than a simple decorative device for visitors, however, once within one of the lands at a Disney park, visitors were completely enveloped within its theme. A themed land was truly a carefully planned and orchestrated imaginary world where visitors could escape the themes of the "real" world.

Within each Disney park themes were chosen to appeal to a wide variety of interests and tastes. Lands which the parks had in common included Main Street, Frontierland, Tomorrowland, Fantasyland, and Adventureland. Encompassed within these were images of the most treasured elements of America's past, the fascinations of technologies which were shaping the future, and the myths which had helped shape the American cultural heritage. The images also were brought to life in a variety of ways. Typically, each land contained adventurous, roller coaster-like rides, more subdued rides where the themes were portrayed and observed in interesting detail, and spectator films and shows. The rides and attractions had been crafted by professional "Imagineers" whose goal was to make each completely unique to the Disney theme park experience.

Another cornerstone of the Disney theme park franchise was the rich heritage of the company's cartoon characters. Developed in films which were re-released roughly every five years to acculturate a new generation of patrons,[23] the characters were active in the theme parks in a variety of ways. Costumed characters roamed the park in search of photo opportunities with young visitors, were the subject of rides and attractions within Fantasyland, and most visitors left the park having purchased some piece of memorabilia which featured the characters.

Disney characters had become staples of the American youth experience. They were colorful, fun, highly visible, and had been merchandised into the psyche of children through ubiquitous product licensing. Disney characters also represented rich experiences which helped account for the depth of their appeal. Included in the cast of characters were: "Mickey Mouse, a scrappy rodent with a 'nice guy' personality; Donald Duck, known for his flights of volcanic but ineffectual rage; Snow White and the Seven Dwarfs, each with his own particular slice of the human condition; Pinocchio, the wooden boy, so easily led astray, and his wise sidekick, Jiminy Crickett; Peter Pan, the perpetual boy; Goofy, the floppy dog full of clumsiness and wild emotion; and scores of pirouetting elephants, dancing skeletons, dandified pirates, and water-toting broomsticks." Each had been born in "ancient tales about what it means to be human, to struggle and bear scars and fight the inner wars—tales that bore the weight of myth."[24] Each, also, was alive, well, and eager to please young theme park customers.

A third element of Disney's success was the unique role that visitors played in the theme park. Once inside the park's gates, visitors were not merely spectators or ride-goers. They were considered by Disney to be participants in a play. Every need and desire was carefully planned for, and frequent interactions with staff were considered an integral part of a visitor's experience. Through the lead of the staff member, in a sense, visitors were drawn into interacting in a particular genre of history or fantasy. In addition, many Disney attractions, such as Tom Sawyer's Island at Disneyland, came to life only through use. Most rides were designed to thrust participants into the heart of the theme itself, so that it could be seen from the inside-out.

Disney's theme parks were continually updated. New rides and attractions were planned every year, and major investments in facilities were made. For instance, in 1991 the company added six new rides and attractions to Walt Disney World, and it soon planned to announce a second theme park at its California site. Some additions were spectacular applications of new ride technologies. Others were based upon new character developments, such as the addition of "Beauty and the Beast" and "The Little Mermaid" stage presentations at the Disney-MGM Studios Theme Park, and a "Muppet Vision 3D" attraction which plunged audiences into the middle of a rowdy Muppets adventure.

Service Delivery

Nothing was left to chance at Disney theme parks. Standards of service, park design and operating details, and human resource policies and practices were integrated to ensure that the Disney "play" would be flawlessly performed day in and day out at each location. Known for its aggressive management of operational details, Disney's stated goal was to exceed its customers expectations every day. As a result, one national survey conducted in 1991 measuring how consumers perceive the quality behind 190 different brand names found that Disney was the most highly regarded brand in the country, surpassing such well known names as Mercedes-Benz, Hallmark, and Rolex.[25] It was one of two service companies listed in the top 15, the other being Cable News Network (CNN).

Service delivery at Disney theme parks had been under constant refinement since the first park opened in 1955. The focal point of the service delivery system was "Disney University," the company's in-house personnel development organization with units specific to each site. Because of the nature of the Disney "play," it was the attitudes and competence of the thousands of Disney park employees which accounted for the experience of visitors. It was at Disney University that new employees were oriented to Disney's strict service standards, received on-going communication and training, and joined for frequent recognition and social events. Conceived in 1955 by Walt Disney, Disney University was opened officially in 1961.

Disney University modeled the attitudes required to re-create the desired level of service in the park. As one Disney University manager put it, "Walt felt that you couldn't have a supervisor yell at you and then walk through the front door and greet a guest as if nothing were wrong. . . . He knew that you need to treat employees in the same way that you want them to treat guests."[26]

Disney's employee population was diverse across its various locations, administrative functions, and creative roles. The majority of Disney theme park employees were young, many of high school and college age. Park workers were paid hourly, and tasks could be routine and repetitive. Still, Disney maintained very high expectations for their performance. Consistent with Disney's entertainment concept, employees were called "cast members," even those who worked "backstage" in operations. They wore "costumes," not uniforms, and were "cast in a role" instead of given job duties. Park visitors were called "guests."

Cast members had to meet stiff dress and grooming requirements. These were communicated to potential employees at initial interview sessions, and Disney relied on self-selection as a first employment screen. Following an initial contact, Disney used a peer interview process to select cast members. Three potential hires would meet with one Disney personnel manager for a 45-minute interview session. Applicants were watched closely for how well they listened to their peers, how well they responded to questions, and whether they smiled and maintained an appropriate attitude.[27]

An extensive orientation program was the first step for both individual cast members and the company's quality assurance efforts. The orientation consisted of indoctrination in Disney's service standards (based on the principles of Safety, Courtesy, Show and Efficiency), classroom instruction in Disney's policies, facilities, resources, and procedures, and extensive on-the-job training. Trainers were themselves cast members who had proven to be exceptional in their roles.

Certain messages were continually reinforced throughout the initial training process. First, it was stressed that happiness was measured differently by every guest and was a challenge to create. Second, trainees learned that customer perceptions were extremely fragile. Finally, it was emphasized that employees were "on stage" at every moment and should look to provide service. As one cast member described, "You don't just make good food and pass it over the counter. It's the idea of extending yourself to guests."[28] In addition, fixing customer problems was given top priority. Employees had wide latitude to "act as a company" when responding to a customer concern.

Employees were evaluated by supervisors based upon their energy, enthusiasm, commitment, and pride. The company maintained a variety of recognition programs for outstanding service delivery, including service recognition awards, milestone banquets for 10, 15, and 20 years of service, and informal recognition parties. Traditionally, the theme parks would re-open for a night during the Christmas Holidays, and management would operate the park for the benefit of cast members and their families. At one such event, Chairman Michael Eisner was on hand to serve hamburgers and hot dogs.

Beyond the management of its cast to provide exceptional service, Disney was religious in managing every detail of its theme parks to exceed customer expectations. For instance, in anticipation of guests from different parts of the country asking questions about the flowers in its Florida park, Disney maintained a small instructional garden outside of its employee cafeteria at the site. Also, each park contained dozens of phones connecting to a central question-and-answer hot line, so that employees could find the answer to any question immediately. An average of 610,000 customer letters were received by Disney every year. Each one was read, and a summary report was written monthly for top management, who acted to correct any significant problems noted. As a final assurance of service quality Disney maintained an active mystery shopping program.[29]

Tokyo Disneyland

Disney products, including films and television shows, had been sold in Western Europe for over 50 years. In 1988 European sales accounted for 25% of all Disney product licensing sales,[30] and in 1991 international revenues accounted for 22% of all Disney revenues. Walt Disney Attractions had a major international presence through Tokyo Disneyland. Officially opened in 1983, attendance at Tokyo Disneyland exceeded 16 million in 1991, a record year, when it also welcomed its 100 millionth guest to the park (25 million guests had attended by August of 1985 and 40 million guests had attended by February of 1988).[31] Attendance had exceeded 10 million during each year of operation. Fiscal year 1990 revenues were $988 million at then current exchange rates.[32]

The Oriental Land Company owned and operated Tokyo Disneyland. Disney designed the park and licensed the use of its characters in return for 10% of admissions revenues and 5% of food and souvenir revenues. At the time of the arrangement, cash generated was used to help fund the Epcot Center, which was under construction. In 1991 discussions were underway between Disney and the Oriental Land Company regarding building a second theme park near the first.

Tokyo Disneyland was considered to be a tremendous success from the time of its opening. It appeared to benefit from a strong Japanese appetite for American styled popular entertainment and an increasing trend in Japan towards leisure. As one American magazine put it, "Japan has always looked to America for its popular culture: James Dean, Levi's, McDonald's. Surfer boys and Madonna's are everywhere. So nobody complained about cultural pollution when Disney's ships sailed into Tokyo Bay."[33]

In 1988 10% of the park's visitors were school children and 75% were repeat visitors, largely from metropolitan Tokyo.[34] The design of the park was virtually identical to Disney's Southern California park, and The Oriental Land company had aggressively added new attractions each year. Virtually all signs and logos in the park were written in English, as were the name badges of cast members. While most cast members primarily spoke Japanese, most live shows and attractions were conducted in English. Of 30 restaurants in the park, only one sold Japanese food. This was because many of the parks older visitors from the Tokyo area had been slower to adapt to the American taste in food. In all other respects, the park was as American as the American parks themselves.

There was some evidence that Tokyo Disneyland was a special cultural haven in Japan, despite stylistic differences between the Disney approach and the Japanese way of life. The company noted that in a country which actively resisted many U.S. products, there was tremendous appeal for Disney's brand of entertainment. This was evident in public transportation leading to and from the park, where normally reserved individuals were openly enthusiastic and usually carried a number of souvenirs.[35]

Also, the company's celebration of New Year's Day markedly broke from Japanese tradition. While the new year is traditionally a serious time within Japan, there was an annual festive party at Disneyland on that day and evening. Extremely popular, the event drew 139,000 visitors in 1991.[36]

Visitor experiences of Tokyo Disneyland were overwhelmingly positive. Comments often revolved around the cleanliness of the park and the efficiency and politeness of staff members. One American tourist familiar with the U.S. theme parks said, "We had great fun. It was exactly the same as the U.S. Disneylands. It was a little funny to see a Japanese Snow White, and the food wasn't very good, but otherwise we thought we were in Florida."[37]

Another tourist commented on locals' fascination with Mickey Mouse. "The shops were mobbed. Everybody buys souvenirs, particularly Mickey Mouse things, and there is a larger selection than in the states. Japanese culture is oriented towards giving gifts, and I think a gift from Disneyland is 'in.' And the people are every bit as good at running the park, even though it was quite crowded. It was so clean it was almost sterile."[38]

An American living in Tokyo accounted for the success of Disneyland in Japan by comparing the Disney experience with Japanese culture. "Young Japanese are very clean cut. They respond well to Disney's clean cut image, and I am sure they had no trouble filling positions. Also, young Japanese are generally comfortable wearing uniforms, obeying their bosses, and being part of a team. These are all parts of the Disney formula."[39]

She added, "Tokyo is very crowded, and Japanese here are used to crowds and waiting lines. They are very patient. And above all Japanese are always very polite to strangers. I have been welcomed into elevators. They give it and expect it, and Disney is a natural." As another observer put it, "Tokyo, Tokyo Disneyland. It's hard to tell where one leaves off and the other starts (parts of Tokyo look more like Tomorrowland than the real thing). This is a match made in Walt Disney's heaven."[40]

Euro Disney

Project Overview

The idea of a European theme park and resort complex had been germinating within Disney since the early 1980s. In 1981, the company began an international bidding process for locating Euro Disney, initially involving Germany, Spain, France and others.[41] It felt that the success of the Tokyo park proved the international appeal of the concept. Spain and France were considered most seriously for the project, which would provide more than 30,000 jobs for the host country.[42] The advantage of Spain was thought to be the weather, and the advantage of France was thought to be its central location.

In 1987 Disney signed an agreement with the French government to locate the complex in the farming community of Marme-la-Vallee, just outside of Paris. The company was highly optimistic that this sight would turn out to be a winner. One reason was the access to the site by the European population, which exceeded that of the United States by 150 million in roughly one-half of the land mass. Seventeen million people lived within two hours of the site by car, 109 million people lived within six hours of the site by car, and 310 million people could reach the complex by plane in less than two hours. The planned opening of the Euro Tunnel in 1994 would make Euro Disney accessible from England in four hours by car.[43]

Secondly, France, and particularly Paris, was already a highly popular vacation destination. Roughly 50 million tourists visited France annually, spending an estimated $21 billion.[44] Also, Disney hoped to benefit from European vacation practices. Europeans typically took upwards of five weeks of vacation a year, whereas most Americans took only two or three.[45] In what looked like a confirmation of Disney's decision, a poll conducted in France in 1988 revealed that 85% of the population welcomed Euro Disney.[46]

Disney down played concerns about the weather in central France, where winter temperatures could reach 23 degrees Farenheit (**Exhibit 3**). Again, Disney pointed to the experience of Japan. "If Tokyo had not taught us that the parks are weatherproof," said Robert Fitzpatrick, "we might have chosen to go to Spain because of the warmer climate."[47] In Tokyo covered waiting lines and additional indoor heat had proved to be adequate buffers against inclement weather. These precautions were planned at Euro Disney, which also added an outdoor skating rink at the Hotel New York for additional winter appeal.

Contractual concessions made by the French government made the project attractive (although Spain had reportedly tabled an even more generous offer). France agreed to extend highways and the metropolitan railway to the site, build a high speed TGV train extension at their own expense, reduce the value-added tax on goods sold from 18.6% to 7%, and provide over $700 million in loans (over $960 million was committed by the end of the project) at the subsidized rate of 7.85%, with no repayment for five years. In addition, France agreed to artificially value the land at $5,000 per acre, its value as agricultural land in 1971, and it guaranteed the valuation for tax purposes for 20 years.[48] This would lower the amount of taxes Disney would pay to local government for services it would provide, such as maintenance of the water supply and fire protection. A portion of the site had been expropriated from local farmers by the French government.[49]

Euro Disney was 49% owned by The Walt Disney Company (42% after adjusting for a convertible bond issue outstanding) and 51% owned by a separate company called Euro Disney S.C.A., which traded on the French Bourse. In accordance with an agreement between Disney and the French government, all shares of Euro Disney were initially offered to European investors. The Walt Disney Company had invested a reported $160 million in the equity of Euro Disney,[50] in which it had three revenue streams in addition to its equity position. These were management fees of 3% of gross revenues for the first five years and 6% thereafter, royalty fees of roughly 7.5% on gross revenues, and a hefty incentive management fee based on the cash flow of the park.

One analyst estimated that Disney would capture 75% to 80% of the pre-tax income of the complex.[51]

Euro Disney financial goals for the first year of operation included attracting 11 million visitors and achieving operating income of $373 million at April 12, 1992 exchange rates[52] (**Exhibit 4**). Euro Disney's financial projections were based upon a detailed study conducted by the consulting firm of Arthur D. Little ("ADL").[53] ADL developed attendance projections and tested the reasonableness of pricing and operating assumptions. Cost estimates largely were determined by comparison with the experience of the other Disney theme parks.

Admission to the park cost $41 for adults and $27 for children at April, 1992 exchange rates. Hotel accommodations ran from $130 per night to $350 per night during the peak season, and roughly 25% less during the off-season. Camp sites cost roughly $47 per night. The Walt Disney Travel Company offered discount travel packages to the complex. The company anticipated visitors would spend roughly $30 on food, merchandise, and parking, per person, per day, growing by 5% annually.[54]

The capacity of the park was 50,000 visitors, and admission gates were closed after this figure was reached.[55] As visitors left the park, then, additional visitors would be admitted for the balance of the afternoon and evening. For instance, on one occasion in the opening three months the gates of the park were closed from 11 A.M. to 3 P.M. because the park had reached capacity, and a large number of additional guests subsequently were admitted.[56] In fact, a Euro Disney spokesman reported in May of 1992, "There have been between 20,000 and 60,000 visitors per day (and) many times there were more than 60,000 per day."[57]

ADL estimated that initial attendance could be as low as 11.7 million visitors and as high as 17.8 million visitors (Disney used a target of 11 million because, as Robert Fitzpatrick put it, "I prefer to under-promise and over-deliver").[58] Subsequent attendance growth was projected to average 2% annually for 20 years, compared to average growth of 3.8% at Disney's other parks.[59]

ADL's methodology involved identifying individual target markets by distance from the site and population, estimating penetration rates for each market, and estimating the average number of annual visits per guest for each market. ADL assumed that the design and scope of Euro Disney would require visitors to either plan extended stays or return trips, and that the capacity and quality of the hotels would encourage this.

Per capita spending assumptions were consistent with Disney's other parks, and ADL considered them to be reasonable, given local market conditions. With respect to admission prices, the firm reviewed prices charged by entertainment options which were considered competitive with Euro Disney. Euro Disney prices were higher than other European theme parks, which were perceived to be of inferior quality. However, they were lower than prices charged in the Paris region for quality adult-oriented entertainment and in line with prices charged for family-oriented attractions. Food and beverage prices also were compared with those of tourist destinations in the Paris region, as well as other theme parks and were found to be reasonable.[60]

The company planned a Phase II of the Euro Disney project, which would include a Disney-MGM Studios Park and an additional 13,000 hotel rooms. Entrance to the second park would require a separate admission ticket, and Euro Disney projected 8 million visitors during its first year of operation.[61] Disney budgeted $3 billion to complete Phase II.[62] Originally planned to open in 1996, at one point Disney moved the opening to "1995 or even 1994."[63] However, following the opening of Euro Disney, the scheduled start date of the second park was set back to 1996.[64] In addition, Disney planned to build out the Marne-la-Vallee site for 25 years. Additional rides and attractions would be built, and the company also planned new office complexes, apartments, and perhaps other residential housing units (**Exhibit 5**).

Theme Park Design

Euro Disney, Phase I, consisted of a theme park and extensive lodging and recreation facilities. The theme park included 29 rides and attractions, and it was somewhat smaller than Disney's Florida parks. The balance was comprised by six themed hotels with 5,200 rooms designed to meet a variety of budgets, a 595-site "Davy Crockett" campground which included 414 cabins, a 27-hole championship golf course, and a variety of restaurants, shops, and live entertainment options, many in the large Festival Disney entertainment center.

The park was intended to continue Disney's traditional design. It shared the themed lands of the other Disney parks and featured most of the same rides and attractions. Still, the design of the complex departed in some ways from the traditional formula in an effort to accommodate the preferences of European guests and certain French cultural requirements. Market research was used to set the tone of the resort. Cultural requirements, involving such things as park design, grooming standards for employees, and eating habits, were expressed by vocal French intellectuals, French government officials, local trade unions, and local press.

Research Disney conducted on European travel to the United States showed that the three things tourists were most interested in seeing were New York, Disneyland, and the western United States. As a result, the complex was the most "Western American" of all of Disney's parks. Three of the six hotel properties, the "Cheyenne," the "Santa Fe," and the "Sequoia Lodge" had distinctly western flavors. An attraction which had been called "The Rivers of America" at other parks was called "The Rivers of the Far West" at Euro Disney, and a ride which in the U.S. and Tokyo had been set in a New Orleans styled mansion was in France set in a mining town of the old west.

The company also responded to concerns that the experience would be too "Americanized." France's intellectual community, particularly of the Left, voiced especially harsh criticisms. They decried what they considered to be the "cultural imperialism" of Euro Disney.[65] They felt it would encourage in France an unhealthy American brand of consumerism. For others, also, Euro Disney became symbols of America within France. On June 28 a group of French farmers blockaded Euro Disney in protest of farm policies the United States supported at the time.[66]

Subsequent to concerns raised by the French government, Disney assured that French would be the first language of the park. Still, most signs would be bilingual, as would be the park's employees. Disney also promoted the benefit of an English speaking destination in France in its American tour literature.

In other respects Disney attempted to imbue the park with a European flavor. In Fantasyland it was stressed that Disney characters had their roots in European mythology. They were portrayed as such in attractions ("European folklore with a Kansas twist," as Michael Eisner called it).[67] The Peter Pan attraction featured Edwardian-style architecture, Snow White had her home in a Bavarian Village, and Cinderella lived in a French Inn. The Alice in Wonderland attraction was surrounded by a 5,000 square foot European hedge maze. In Discoveryland Euro Disney featured tributes to European Renaissance heros and to France's Jules Verne. Adventureland would invoke the imagination of famous European adventure tales such as Sinbad the Sailor, Arabian Nights, and the Thief of Baghdad.

A number of other concerns relating to the design of the park had been expressed in the French press. One of the most noted was a flap over Disney's decision not to serve wine at the park, consistent with its policies in the U.S. and Tokyo. It was felt by many that this was a departure from important French tradition and lunch habits, as well as a snub to the country's reputation for excellence in wine making. Visitors who wanted alcoholic beverages congregated at Festival Disney, an entertainment complex outside of the theme park and adjacent to the Hotel New York. There they were "supervised by unsmiling security men and CRS riot police with guns."[68]

Disney addressed a concern that French visitors would not tolerate long waiting lines. The company planned films and other entertainment diversions for guests in line for a ride. Some also pointed out differences between European and American eating habits. They pointed out that Europeans were not accustomed to eating fast meals at off hours, sometimes while walking, as were Americans, and predicted that dining facilities would have problems serving peak demands. A small sample of visitors to Euro Disney confirmed that this had, indeed, become a problem, although they did not cite it specifically as a cause of dissatisfaction with the park.[69]

In anticipation of concerns about food, Euro Disney featured foods from around the world at its many themed restaurants and snack bars. This was in contrast to the strictly American flavor of Tokyo Disneyland. Disney also claimed that the food was of higher quality than at its other parks. In an effort to boldly demonstrate its claim, Disney even invited top Paris chefs to visit and taste it. Visitors to Euro Disney could not confirm a marked improvement in the food, however.[70]

While Euro Disney was controversial in the French press, not all French intellectuals criticized Disney. For instance, philosopher Michel Serres noted, "It is not America that is invading us. It is we who adore it, who adopt its fashions and above all, its words."[71] For his own part, a French critic who had been vocal in his opposition to Euro Disney did publicly lament that his young son loved Disney characters.[72]

Another American observer responded to the controversy by saying that "Euro Disney is an imaginary place, a culture without sin," and he commended American culture for producing such creativity.[73] Euro Disney's Robert Fitzpatrick took a somewhat more combative tact when he said, "We didn't come in and say 'O.K., we're going to put a beret and a baguette on Mickey Mouse. . . .' We are who we are."[74]

The Start Up Process

Disney met a monumental challenge in readying the park for its April 12 start date, which involved completion of the second largest construction project in the history of Europe, as well as preparing operationally for the launch. In addition to the task of marketing the park, Disney hired and trained 14,000 employees to fill 12,000 jobs in anticipation of the opening.[75] Another 5,000 temporary jobs were filled by the peak July season.[76]

Euro Disney was aggressively marketed by Disney as well as other firms. Disney successfully encouraged dozens of articles on the complex in magazines throughout Europe. Prior to the opening it sent a model of The Sleeping Beauty Castle around Europe to dramatically publicize the park. An extensive Europe-wide ad campaign was launched to market the opening celebration, which was broadcast live across Europe. In addition, Swiss food giant Nestle sponsored extensive cross-promotions of Euro Disney at its own expense.[77]

Perhaps the biggest challenge was preparing operationally to provide Disney's standard of customer service. To accomplish this task, Robert Fitzpatrick announced that a leading priority was to indoctrinate all employees in the Disney service philosophy, in addition to training them in operational policies and procedures.[78]

Disney opened a special center at Euro Disney's new Disney University in September of 1991. Its goal was to select 10,000 employees within six months while maintaining selective applicant-to-hire ratios. A staff of 60 interviewers had been assembled for that purpose.[79] Stated selection criteria were applicant friendliness, warmth, and liking of people. The company attempted to hire employees of nationalities proportional to expected visitor counts. Its initial objective was to hire 45% French employees, 30% other European, and 15% from outside of Europe,[80] but by opening day the cast was 70% French.[81] Europe had recently entered a recession, in which it remained at the time of opening, making it somewhat easier to attract an applicant pool. Most cast members were paid roughly $6.50 an hour at April 12, 1992 exchange rates, which was 15% above France's minimum wage, and shifts were generally 169 hours per month.[82]

At the same time Disney aggressively cross-trained managers and supervisors to ensure service quality. Prior to opening, 270 managers were cross-trained in the Disney methods at the company's other three theme parks. Also, another 200 managers were imported from the other parks to work at Euro Disney.[83]

Disney encountered difficult resistance in the hiring process, for which it was criticized by applicants, the press, and French unions. The controversy revolved around Disney's grooming requirements. Disney strictly enforced a dress code, a ban on facial hair, a ban on colored stockings, standards for neat hair and fingernails, and a policy of "appropriate undergarments." However, applicants and labor leaders in France felt the requirements were excessive, being much stricter than the requirements of other employers. They hoped to force the company to loosen its standards, but they were unsuccessful.[84]

Another problem Disney faced was that of staff housing. The agricultural Marne-La-Vallee did not have apartment space for the thousands of Disney's workers at the complex, and the jobs generally did not pay well enough to make decent Parisian housing affordable. At the time of the opening an estimated 4,000 staff members were affected by the housing shortage. By building its own apartments and renting rooms in local homes, Disney was adding rooms at a rate of 100 per week.[85]

Disney successfully staffed and trained cast members for the complex by the time of the opening. However, within the first nine weeks of operation roughly 1,000 employees left Euro

Disney, about one-half of whom left voluntarily.[86] Under French employment law an employee could be terminated during their first two years with little difficulty, but after the two year period performance documentation, notification requirements, and severance requirements became stringent. The long hours and hectic pace of work at the park were cited as the reasons for the turnover. "A lot went because it was chaotic at first," said one English waitress.[87] Disney conceded that employees had worked under "tough conditions" at the time of opening.[88]

One example of a cast member who left was a 22-year-old medical student from a nearby town who signed up for a weekend job. After one weekend of "brainwashing," as he called it, and one weekend of training, he went to work at a Fantasyland shop. One day during his first weekend he worked 11 "frantic" hours straight, and by the next weekend the entire shop personnel had changed. He left after a dispute with his supervisor over the timing of his lunch break.[89]

Another cast member, a waiter in one of the better hotels, blamed communications problems between supervisors and workers for the difficulties. "I don't think they realized what Europeans were like," he said, "that we ask questions and don't think all the same." Still, he added that "it's getting better; they're listening more to the staff."[90]

Visitor Reactions

From a small polling sample visitor experiences of Euro Disney were mixed. Many visitors found in Euro Disney everything for which they had hoped. Others complained that the park did not meet the U.S. standard, suffering from long lines, poor service, and operational glitches.

One family which had driven in from northern Europe was thrilled with the experience, because they were able to interact with the Disney characters they had always revered. They said they could never afford to come to the United States to do so. Another visitor from nearby Paris was simply impressed by the scale of the complex. He had already visited the complex twice in its first three months of operation.[91]

As reported in the French press, an 11-year-old visitor named Vincent exclaimed, "I loved everything. There was nothing I didn't like." Thirteen-year-old Cyndie said, "I asked my parents if we can come back. We just didn't have enough time to see everything."[92] In addition, after opening day one London newspaper reported that a group of German visitors had all "had a great time," despite considerable frustration with waiting lines.[93]

Others were not as impressed, however. Themes echoed by visitors less enthusiastic with Euro Disney included a lack of appreciation of cast member performance, the difficulties associated with the multi-cultural nature of the park, and the high cost of a day at the park. In addition, a number of observers noted that Euro Disney represented a departure from a traditional French entertainment experience.

One British journalist wrote, "Cast members taken on to work at Euro Disney are mostly nice enough. 'Mostly,' because even on opening weekend some clearly couldn't care less. . . . My overwhelming impression of the. . .employees was that they were out of their depth. There is much more to being a cast member than endlessly saying 'bonjour.' Apart from having a detailed knowledge of the site, Euro Disney staff have the anxiety of not knowing in what language they are going to be addressed. . . . Many were struggling. One cast member, who has worked for the company in the U.S., candidly volunteered that service at Euro Disney falls way short of the standards at the American parks."[94]

An American visitor to the park agreed that the experience fell short of what she had come to expect from Disney. "They compete with their own high standards," she said, "but they are not winning in France. Most of the workers are simply not aiming to please, even though they are thrilled to have jobs in the rotten economy. They are playing a different game than their American counterparts. They are acting like real people instead of 'Disney' people. Unfortunately, you get the feeling that the whole thing is not yet under control."[95]

Another American visitor voiced concerns over the international flavor of Euro Disney. "The park has kind of a strange feel to it. They haven't yet figured out whether it is going to be an American park, a French park, or a European park. This is in the atmosphere of the park itself, and it is compounded by the behavior of visitors from various parts of Europe, which can be quite different. Little things like the attitudes of different nationalities with respect to disposing of trash are very noticeable. And differences in waiting-line behavior is striking. For instance, Scandinavians appear quite content to wait for rides, whereas some of the southern Europeans seem to have made an Olympic event out of getting to the ticket taker first." He went on to describe that there generally was considerable restlessness with extensive waiting lines, even though he did not perceive the park to be terribly crowded (on crowded weekend days visitors complained that lines averaged between one and two hours for rides which they perceived to average 10 to 15 minutes in length). However, he added that "even at its worst the service at Euro Disney was better than the best I encountered in Paris."[96]

The difficulties in accommodating the cultural diversity of the complex were also noted by the popular press. In a report on the opening of Euro Disney one newspaper asked, "Can an American theme park in Europe please all ages and nationalities? And in what country, if any, is this fantasy never-never-land which started with a Hollywood mouse? It is not, except in the most literal sense, France."[97] British advertising executive David Moutrie agreed. He observed, "I think as far as the management is concerned (Euro Disney) just happens to be in the middle of Europe handy for a big population. If somebody said to me when we get back, 'have you been to France?' I'd be tempted to say no."[98]

On this theme, some observers felt that the idea of Euro Disney was out of character for the French population. Comments included claims that many French were too individualistic and private to appreciate the standardized and crowded Disney theme park experience. Others felt that the French tended to enjoy entertainment which was more intellectual in nature than Euro Disney.[99]

And not only were there questions of whether Disney could be enjoyed by the local population, but some also felt that it was the character of the European labor force, rather than experience or training, which would account for less than perfect service at Euro Disney. Wrote one journalist, "The Disney style of service is one with which Americans have grown up. There are several styles of service (or lack of it) in Europe, unbridled enthusiasm is not a marked feature of them."[100]

The cost of the experience was thought to be an issue for some. While little dissatisfaction with admissions prices among those in attendance at the park was reported, it was reported that many French visitors knew people who had been deterred from coming by the cost.[101] There were also grumbles about the cost of Disney souvenirs. "I refuse to pay Ffr49 (roughly $9) for a little Mickey Mouse statue," said one representative Parisian visitor.[102]

For its own part, Disney acknowledged that it was still working out the details of its operations. It felt that it was unreasonable to expect a project of the size of Euro Disney to be perfect. As one senior Euro Disney manager put it, "You don't get it right the second you start."[103]

Decisions

There was precedent for believing that a rocky start was not catastrophic in the theme park business.   Universal's Florida theme park had had a disastrous opening due to technical difficulties, but it quickly rebounded and was considered successful. Euro Disney was far from a disaster. It was too early to tell what the impact of poor fall and winter weather would be, but the attendance figure of over 30,000 per day was respectable. If this number were annualized, then Euro Disney's projection of 11 million visitors during the first year of operation would be met. Although the local French population had not attended as planned (the company claimed that Parisians were "postponing their visits" until the fall), visitation from the rest of Europe was running higher than planned.

Profitability was another matter.   Even if revenues could be brought in line with projections for the balance of the year, the announcement that the park would not be profitable for the five and one-half months ending September 30 was sobering news (analysts estimated that the losses could be as high as $60 million).[104] Observers could not assess with certainty whether the shortfall was due to the level at which the company geared up operations, as it claimed, or some other set of reasons. Whatever the cause, the poor profit picture would constrain Euro Disney's options for fixing any operating problems it had and initiating programs to bring in visitors.

The coming winter months were clearly critical to Euro Disney's chances for financial success. Here, also, there was cause for concern. Prior to 1987 (the last time such information was made publicly available), an average of 65% to 70% of attendance at the warm weather U.S. parks came during the April through September period.[105] Accordingly, one knowledgeable U.S. analyst estimated that seven million of the complex's projected 11 million visitors would attend in the five and one-half months from the opening to the September 30 fiscal year end.[106] Travel agents representing Euro Disney reported that, while demand was very strong for the balance of the summer months, advance bookings for the end of the year were much lower.[107] Analysts estimated that hotel room occupancy was running at 90% during the July peak season, and they estimated occupancy had averaged 68% for the April to July period.[108] On the other hand, one travel agent reported that less than 20% of its projected September bookings, 12% of its projected November bookings, and 10% of its projected December bookings had materialized. Other agents were in similar situations.[109]

Agents did not know whether to attribute the low level of forward bookings to lack of advance planning or more fundamental problems with the park, because they lacked experience against which to benchmark. Moreover, even if travel to Euro Disney declined, local visitation could pick up the slack. Perhaps waiting-line-cautious French simply planned to wait for crowds to thin.

Even as summer was at its peak Euro Disney management took actions to improve its attendance outlook and profit position. By the time of its opening, Euro Disney had slashed rates at its least expensive hotels by 25%. In July it confirmed that some rooms were being offered at $73 a night for the winter season at current exchange rates.[110] On July 31 it was reported that the Walt Disney Company, headquartered in Burbank, California, would slash 300 to 400 jobs from its Imagineering unit. It cited the completion of Euro Disney, Phase I as the reason that such a cut was possible.[111] Presumably, then, a portion of the cost savings would be passed on to Euro Disney.

Euro Disney management still faced serious issues. Not the least of these was prioritizing its objectives in the face of a somewhat conflicting problem set, consisting of an uncertain revenue outlook, cost problems, and mixed reviews of its service delivery system. Compounding Euro Disney's situation was the fact that it appeared to be in the spotlight of the national and international press. Given the controversies which swirled around the opening of the park, its every action could prove to be newsworthy.

One set of decisions facing Euro Disney concerned getting the service system up to the standards and cost levels of the other Disney parks. Such issues as waiting lines, consistent cast member courtesy, and employee turnover deserved immediate attention. While practice would surely help, perhaps there were other things Euro Disney could do to speed the process.
A second set of decisions was the marketing of the park to achieve winter attendance targets, particularly in light of the visibility of Disney's critics in France. It needed to find a way to promote the park in such a way that there would be minimum of costs in terms of public relations. Pricing, communications, special events, and tie-ins with other parts of The Walt Disney Company were all levers available to Euro Disney management.

Finally, Disney had planned major investments in Phase II of the park. The level, timing, and nature of the investments still were at issue. Perhaps there were significant lessons to be learned from the Phase I experience which Disney could apply to Phase II and improve its chances for success. Issues Disney would surely review in planning for Phase II would be whether the adaptation of the Disney entertainment concept to European, and specifically French, culture had been over done or under done, and whether its management policies and training methods had been appropriate to its task.

Exhibit 1   The Walt Disney Company Financial Summary (in $ millions, except Return on Equity percentages)

	1991	1990	1989	1988
Revenues	$6,182	$5,843	$4,594	$3,438
Net income	637	824	703	522
Return on equity	17%	25%	26%	25%
Capital spending	1,425	1,352	1,414	1,043

Sources: The Walt Disney Company Annual Report, 1991; The Walt Disney Company Fact Book, 1991

Exhibit 2   The Walt Disney Segment Financial Data (in $ millions)

	1991	1990	1989	1988
Revenues				
Theme parks, resorts	$2,865	$3,020	$2,595	$2,042
Filmed entertainment	2,593	2,250	1,588	1,149
Consumer products	724	574	411	247
Operating Income				
Theme parks, resorts	617	889	785	565
Filmed entertainment	318	313	257	186
Consumer products	230	223	187	134

Source: The Walt Disney Company Annual Report, 1991

Exhibit 3   Marne-la-Vallee Seasonal Weather Averages: Average Temperatures and Rainfall (Degrees Farenheit)

	High	Low	Rainy Days
Winter	49	27	16
Spring	58	33	16
Summer	73	58	12
Fall	60	48	14

Source: The Harper Collins Guide to Euro Disneyland 1992

Note: A rain day may be a full or partial day of rain.

Exhibit 4   Euro Disney Financial Projections (in $ millions)[a]

	1992	1993	1994	1995
Revenues				
Magic Kingdom[b]	$ 774.8	$ 849.8	$ 985.5	$1,068.1
Resort development	226.6	391.2	642.3	926.5
Total revenues	1,000.4	1,241.0	1,624.8	1,994.6
Operating Expenses				
Magic Kingdom[b]	482.3	517.6	576.8	615.0
Resort development	145.3	273.9	443.6	542.0
Total operating expenses	627.6	791.5	1,020.4	1,157.0
Operating Income	372.8	449.5	604.4	837.6
Other Expenses				
Royalties	55.1	60.8	70.6	77.0
Management incentive fees	10.0	31.2	87.0	175.7
Other	243.6	244.7	297.1	279.0
Pretax profit	61.1	112.8	149.7	305.9

[a]Converted at April 12, 1992 exchange rate of Ffr 5.48:$1.

[b]Includes theme park and 500 room Disneyland Hotel.

Exhibit 5   Euro Disney Property Development Plans (units listed, except as noted)

	Phase I	Long-Term	Total
Theme parks	1	1	2
Hotel rooms	5,200	13,000	18,200
Campsite plots	595	1,505	2,100
Entertainment center[a]	22,000	38,000	60,000
Office space[a]	30,000	670,000	700,000
Corporate park[a]	50,00	700,000	750,000
Golf courses	1	1	2
Single family homes	570	1,930	2,500
Retail shopping space[a]		95,000	95,000
Water recreation area	1	1	
Multi-family homes		3,000	3,000
Time-share units		2,400	2,400

[a]In square meters.

Source: S. G. Warburg Securities, "Euro Disneyland S.C.A.: Offer for Sale", October 5, 1989
            Prospectus

Endnotes

[1]   The Walt Disney Company Annual Report (1991)

[2]   "Only the French Elite Scorn Mickey's Debut," (*New York Times*, April 13, 1992).

[3]   op. cit.

[4]   "Euro Disney Draws Over 1.5 Million in First 7 Weeks" (*Wall Street Journal*, June 10, 1992).

[5]   ibid.

[6]   "Euro Disney Sees Loss; Disney Profit Rises 33%" (*New York Times*, July 24, 1992).

[7]   "Mickey Mouse Diplomacy" (*Minneapolis Star Tribune*, June 19, 1992).

[8]   "Playing Disney in the Parisian Fields" (*New York Times*, February 17, 1991).

[9]   "Euro Disney Draws Over 1.5 Million in First 7 Weeks" (*Wall Street Journal*, June 10, 1992).

[10]   "Mickey Mouse Lures the Stars in Paris" (*London Financial Times*, April 11/April 12, 1992).

[11]   The Walt Disney Company Annual Report (1991).

[12]   "The Walt Disney Company Fact Book" (August 31, 1991).

[13]   ibid.

[14]   The Walt Disney Company Annual Report (1991).

[15]   Joe Flower, *Prince of the Magic Kingdom: Michael Eisner and the Re-Making of Disney* (John Wiley and Sons, Inc., New York, 1991).

[16]   The Walt Disney Company Annual Report (1991).

[17]   "Culture shock for the Mickey Mouse outfit" (London Financial Times, April 23, 1992).

[18]   Joe Flower, *Prince of the Magic Kingdom: Michael Eisner and the Re-Making of Disney* (John Wiley and Sons, New York, 1991).

[19]   "The Walt Disney Company Fact Book," (August 31, 1991).

[20]   op. cit.

[21]   ibid.

[22]   The Walt Disney Company Annual Report (1991).

[23]   David J. Collis, "The Walt Disney Company" (Harvard Business School Case #2-388-147, 1988).

24   Joe Flower, *Prince of the Magic Kingdom: Michael Eisner and the Re-Making of Disney* (New York, John Wiley and Sons, 1991).

25.   "Disney Tops Poll of Best Brand Names" (Los Angeles Times, July 10, 1991).

26.   Charlene Marmer Solomon, "How Does Disney Do It?" (*Personnel Journal*, December 1989).

27.   ibid.

28.   ibid.

29.   ibid.

30.   The Walt Disney Company Annual Report (1988).

31.   The Walt Disney Company Annual Report (1991).

32.   "Playing Disney in the Parisian Fields" (*New York Times*, February 17, 1991).

33.   "Tokyo: Mickey's First Trip Abroad" (*Travel and Leisure*, August 1992).

34.   The Walt Disney Company Annual Report (1988).

35.   The Walt Disney Company Annual Report (1987).

36.   "Tokyo: Mickey's First Trip Abroad" (*Travel and Leisure*, August 1992).

37.   Case Writer Interview, July 1992.

38.   ibid.

39.   ibid.

40.   "Tokyo: Mickey's First Trip Abroad" (*Travel and Leisure*, August 1992).

41.   "Mickey Does Marne-la-Vallee" (*Invest in France Agency*, May 1992).

42.   "Monsieur Mickey or Senor Miqui? Disney Seeks a European Site" (*Business Week*, July 15, 1985).

43.   S.G. Warburg Securities, "Euro Disneyland S.C.A.: Offer for Sale" (October 5, 1989).

44.   "Monsieur Mickey" (*Time Magazine*, March 25, 1991).

45.   Alan S. Gould, "Euro Disney S.C.A." (Dean Witter Equity Research, June 12, 1992).

46.   "Mickey Hops the Pond" (*The Economist*, March 28, 1987).

47.   "Playing Disney in the Parisian Fields," (*New York Times*, February 17, 1991).

48.   Joe Flower, *Prince of the Magic Kingdom: Michael Eisner and the Re-Making of Disney* (John Wiley and Sons, New York, 1991).

49.   "Will French Culture Make Room for Mouse?" (*Minneapolis Star Tribune*, May 19, 1991).

50.   "Playing Disney in the Parisian Fields," (*New York Times* February 17, 1991).

51.   Alan S. Gould, "Euro Disney S.C.A." (Dean Witter Equity Research, June 12, 1992).

52.   S.G. Warburg Securities, "Euro Disneyland S.C.A.: Offer for Sale" (October 5, 1989).

53.   S.G. Warburg Securities, "Euro Disneyland S.C.A.: Offer for Sale" (October 5, 1989).

54.   "Euro Disneyland S.C.A.: Offer for Sale," S.G. Warburg Securities (October 5, 1989).

55.   "Mickey Does Marne-La-Vallee" (Invest in France Agency, May 1992).

56.   "Queuing for Flawed Fantasy" (*London Financial Times*, June 12/June 13, 1992).

57.   op. cit.

58.   Alan S. Gould, "Euro Disney S.C.A." (Dean Witter Equity Research, June 18, 1992).

59.   S.G. Warburg Securities, "Euro Disneyland: Offer for Sale" (October 5, 1989).

60.   ibid.

61.   ibid.

62.   "Playing Disney in the Parisian Fields" (*New York Times*, February 17, 1991).

63.   Euro Disneyland Annual Report (1990).

64.   Alan S. Gould, "Euro Disney S.C.A." (Dean Witter Equity Research, June 12, 1992).

65.   "Only the French Elite Scorn Mickey's Debut" (*New York Times*, April 13, 1992).

66.   "French Farmers Blockade Euro Disneyland," (*Investors Business Daily*, June 29, 1992).

67.   op. cit.

68.   "Queuing for Flawed Fantasy" (*London Financial Times*, June 13/June 14, 1992).

69.   Case Writer Interviews, July 1992.

70.   ibid.

71.   "Only the French Elite Scorn Mickey's Debut" (*New York Times*, April 13, 1992).

72. "As Euro Disney Braces For Its Grand Opening, The French Go Goofy" (*Wall Street Journal*, April 1992).

73. "The French Turn Up Their Noses at Disney? Well, Excuse Mouse!" (*Minneapolis Star Tribune*, April 26, 1992).

74. Associated Press (May 19, 1991).

75. "Disney's Cast of Thousands" (*London Financial Times*, February 18, 1991).

76. "Euro Disney Sees Loss; Disney Profit Rises 33%" (*New York Times*, July 24, 1992).

77. "Disney Gets Many Helping Hands To Sell the New Euro Disneyland" (*Wall Street Journal*, April 1, 1992).

78. Euro Disneyland Annual Report (1990).

79. "Disney's Cast of Thousands" (*London Financial Times*, February 18, 1992).

80. "Continent Will Get Goofy (and Mickey and Donald) with Euro Disney Opening" (*Minneapolis Star Tribune*, March 29, 1992).

81. "Mickey Does Marne-la-Vallee" (Invest in France Agency, May 1992).

82. "Queueing for Flawed Fantasy," *London Financial Times* (June 13/June 14, 1992).

83. Euro Disneyland Annual Report (1990).

84. "Costume Requirements at Euro Disneyland Called a Mickey Mouse Idea" (*Minneapolis Star Tribune*, March 10, 1991).

85. "Queuing for Flawed Fantasy" (*London Financial Times*, June 12/June 13, 1992).

86. "Euro Disney's Fitzpatrick Denies Report That 3,000 Workers Quit Over Low Pay" (*The Wall Street Journal*, May 27, 1992).

87. op. cit.

88. "Euro Disney's Fitzpatrick Denies Report That 3,000 Workers Quit Over Low Pay" (*The Wall Street Journal*, May 27, 1992).

89. "Queuing for Flawed Fantasy" (*London Financial Times* June 13/June 14, 1992).

90. ibid.

91. Case Writer interview.

92. "Euro Disney: Oui or Non?" (*Travel and Leisure*, August 1992).

93. "Queuing for Flawed Fantasy" (*London Financial Times*, June 12/June 13, 1992).

94.   Case Writer interview, July 1992.

95.   ibid.

96.   op. cit.

97.   "Queuing for Flawed Fantasy" (*London Financial Times*, June 13/June 14, 1992).

98.   ibid.

99.   Case Writer interview, July 1992.

100.   "Mickey Mouse Outfit Suffers Culture Shock" (*London Financial Times*, April 23, 1992).

101.   "Queuing for Flawed Fantasy" (*London Financial Times*, June 13/June 14, 1992).

102.   ibid.

103.   "Culture Shock for the Mickey Mouse Outfit" (*London Financial Times*, April 23, 1992).

104.   "Euro Disney Sees Loss; Disney Profit Rises 33%" (*New York Times*, July 24, 1992).

105.   The Walt Disney Company Quarterly Reports.

106.   Alan S. Gould, "Euro Disney S.C.A.," (Dean Witter Equity Research, June 18, 1992).

107.   "A Question of the Mouse's Attraction" (*London Financial Times*, June 12/June 13, 1992).

108.   "Euro Disney Sees Loss; Disney Profit Rises 33%" (*New York Times*, July 24, 1992).

109.   op. cit.

110.   op. cit.

111.   "Lay Offs Loom at Disney" (*Boston Globe*, July 31, 1992).

HARVARD
BUSINESS
SCHOOL
PUBLISHING

2075
JUNE 1, 2007

WENDY STAHL

The Fashion Channel

Introduction

Dana Wheeler, senior vice president of marketing for The Fashion Channel (TFC), sat in her Chicago office and scrolled through the email messages in her inbox. Thankfully, none required an urgent reply. She toggled over to her calendar: no meetings for the rest of the day. Finally, she could focus her thoughts on reviewing her recommendations for TFC's new segmentation and positioning strategy.

Wheeler believed that she had prepared a solid analysis; she felt confident about the strategy she was proposing. But next week's senior management meeting would mark her first big presentation to the company's leaders since she had joined TFC, and, she admitted to herself, she was eager to gain the support of her colleagues.

There was a lot riding on the outcome of this meeting, both for Wheeler and for the channel. If founder and CEO Jared Thomas and his team liked what they heard, Wheeler would move forward to implement her recommendations. The company needed to strengthen its competitive position and would be spending more than $60 million in all national and affiliate advertising, promotion, and public relations in 2007, based on these recommendations. This would be an increase of $15 million over 2006 spending.

Background

TFC was a successful cable TV network– and the only network dedicated solely to fashion, with up-to-date and entertaining features and information broadcast 24 hours per day, 7 days per week. Founded in 1996 by two entrepreneurs, it had experienced constant revenue and profit growth above the industry average almost since the beginning. Revenues for 2006 were forecast at $310.6 million, marking another steady upswing.

Wendy Stahl prepared this case solely as a basis for class discussion and not as an endorsement, a source of primary data, or an illustration of effective or ineffective management. Wendy Stahl is vice president of corporate development at creditcards.com. She received her MBA from Harvard Business School

This case, though based on real events, is fictionalized, and any resemblance to actual persons or entities is coincidental. There are occasional references to actual companies in the narration.

The channel was also one of the most widely available niche networks, reaching almost 80 million U.S. households that subscribed to cable and satellite television.[1] Women between 35 and 54 years were its most avid viewers, according to its annual demographic survey. But beyond basic demographics, the channel didn't have much in the way of detailed information about its viewers. Nor did it attempt to market to any viewer segments in particular. From the beginning, in fact, Jared Thomas had believed that TFC's marketing messages should appeal to as broad a group as possible in order to achieve the highest possible viewership numbers. Early on, the network had chosen "Fashion for Everyone" as the theme for its marketing programs; one of its more popular series in 2005 had been "Look Great on Saturday Night for Under $100."

TFC had clearly grown quickly without articulating any detailed segmentation, branding, or positioning strategy. However, at the beginning of 2006, the network realized that other networks were taking note of its success and beginning to add fashion-related programming to their line-ups. TFC was facing competition that could provide meaningful choices to both viewers and advertisers. By June 2006, these new competitive dynamics had prompted Thomas to rethink his approach to marketing. At the quarterly executive meeting that month, he told his senior team: "It's time for us to build a modern brand strategy and secure The Fashion Channel's position as the market leader. I want to use marketing to lay a foundation for future growth." At the same meeting, Thomas had announced plans to sharply increase TFC's investment in advertising and to hire an experienced marketer to develop marketing and brand-building programs to support TFC's continued growth.

Enter Dana Wheeler, in July 2006. Wheeler had a strong background in marketing for packaged consumer products as well as broad experience in the advertising industry. Thomas expected that Wheeler would draw on these strengths to help TFC build on the momentum it had created to date and stave off any competitors trying to make inroads. Still, he and some of the other members of the leadership team felt an urge to resist change. The network had been highly successful to date and no one wanted to "break something that isn't broken."

Wheeler's Plans

Wheeler turned back to her computer, opened up the slide-deck presentation she had created, and started reviewing it. As she began to page through the materials, she was thinking about the trends in the advertising marketplace that Norm Frazier had been talking about in the sales forecasting meeting this morning.

Frazier, senior vice president of Advertising Sales, had warned that TFC might need to drop the price for a unit of advertising next year by 10% or more if the network did not make some changes in its performance. He mentioned that both Lifetime and CNN had launched fashion-specific programming blocks that were achieving notable ratings (**Exhibit 1**). Frazier was a high-energy salesman who had personally built the strong ad sales performance of the channel. He was justifiably worried. Wheeler had left that meeting acutely aware that next week's executive session wasn't coming a moment too soon.

Wheeler knew that in order to hold or increase price it would be crucial to attract a critical mass of viewers who were interested in the network's content and were also attractive to advertisers. The key would be targeting the right viewers and offering advertisers an attractive mix of viewers when compared with what competitors were offering. Wheeler believed she had good market data that would give her insights into the options for identifying the right segments for TFC. At the same time,

---

[1] There were a total of 110 million households with televisions in the United States. Of those, approximately 70 million TV households subscribed to cable television service.

BRIEF CASES | **HARVARD BUSINESS SCHOOL PUBLISHING**

she knew that the network needed to maintain its overall audience ratings with the cable consumers and the cable affiliate distribution network. If the network changed its offerings in a way that disappointed too many cable subscribers, it could risk losing its distribution support.

Wheeler clicked to the slide that outlined the marketing tools in her arsenal, and then clicked to a slide near the end of the presentation that revealed an aggressive implementation schedule. Her plan was to build a strategy for segmentation, and use it as a base to employ all of the marketing tools—traditional and internet advertising, public relations and promotions—to reach the target consumers with integrated positioning messages. She also knew that it would take time to create and launch all the elements of a well-integrated marketing program and that there was no time to waste.

She moved back a dozen slides or so, opening the ones that summarized TFC's revenue stream from advertising sales and the slides that considered its revenue stream from cable-affiliate fees. Thomas and the rest of the senior management team knew this data as well as she did, she assumed. Everyone felt that advertising was TFC's primary growth opportunity. She wanted to think about her key messages one more time to ensure her recommendations would support building revenues as aggressively as possible.

TFC's Advertising Revenue Model

First, she reviewed TFC's advertising revenue model. TFC was on target to generate $230.6 million in 2006 from advertising. The advertising business model was built on attracting a mix of male and female viewers on a regular basis as measured by "ratings" (the percentage of television households watching on average during a measured viewing period.) Across the entire schedule, TFC's average rating was 1.0. With 110 million television households in the United States, this meant that on average 1,100,000 people were watching at any point in time.[2]

TFC's Ad Sales team sold access to these viewers via advertising spots (30 or 60 seconds in length) to a variety of well-known consumer marketers ranging from cosmetics companies to brand name clothing designers and automobile manufacturers. There were usually six minutes of national ad time in each half hour of programming, 24 hours per day for a total of 2,016 minutes per week. Wheeler knew from industry studies that, in 2006, U.S. consumer advertisers spent almost $20 billion buying spots on cable networks such as TFC. Because there were several hundred cable networks competing for viewers and the related ad dollars, competition for ad revenue was always fierce across all the networks.

While competition was intense for advertising overall, TFC remained the only network dedicated to fashion programming 24 hours per day, 7 days per week. This set up an interesting competitive dynamic. TFC needed to compete against a broad range of networks for advertising revenues. For these networks the ad buyers would be most interested in buying ratings and demographics, and less interested in specific programming subjects. At the same time TFC competed against other fashion-oriented programming that would appeal to advertisers who specifically wanted to participate in that programming context. The strong fashion programming blocks on Lifetime and CNN represented a double-edged competitive challenge. And if successful, more networks would likely copy the concept, skimming more viewers and ad dollars from TFC.

---

[2] The ratings metric is used for all television networks and is calculated on the base of *all* TV households, not the smaller base of cable households. While some networks are not available in all households, the ratings calculation formula does not change but remains Viewers/Total TV HH = Ratings. This standardizes the rating metric used in measuring audiences for advertising purposes.

Dana reminded herself about the conversation she'd had with Norm Frazier about advertising pricing. The network based ad unit prices on several factors, which advertisers also monitored, including the number of viewers (ratings), the audience's characteristics (age, demographics, and lifestyle), and general competitive trends. Prices were expressed as CPM (cost per thousand), which represented the price that an advertiser would pay for an "impression," or moment of viewing.[3] The ad market was dynamic because of the relatively fixed supply of advertising on traditional television networks. Market pricing moved up and down frequently, as advertisers developed new campaigns that required television support. And, in recent years, the advertising buying process had become very sophisticated, with many buying agencies and clients using combinations of surveys and "optimizer" programs to analyze the demographic and psychographic characteristics of audience groups and then establish pricing parameters that fit the audiences various networks delivered. The output of these programs would be a recommended advertising placement portfolio for a specific product campaign.

Networks were increasingly evaluated on their ability to deliver specific target groups. Generally, networks whose audiences were older or had low family incomes commanded lower rates for advertising. Advertisers would pay a premium CPM to reach certain other groups; in 2006, these were men of all ages and women aged 18-34. By increasing the ratings in highly valued demographic groups, the TFC Ad Sales team could achieve CPM pricing increases from 25% to 75%. By attracting a large number of highly valued viewers, the network had the opportunity to substantially grow its advertising revenues.

Cable Affiliate Fees

Wheeler next turned to the slides that dealt with the cable affiliate fee revenue stream. Cable affiliate fees, which were on track to bring in $80 million in 2006, were the second source of TFC revenue. Most U.S. households subscribed to cable television through local affiliates of a large cable multi-system operator (nationally, Comcast, Time Warner, Cablevision, and Cox were the largest). Consumers paid a monthly fee for a basic lineup of channels and incremental fees for premium channels and on-demand programming. TFC was positioned as a basic channel, so most consumers received it automatically when they signed up for basic cable service.

Large multi-system operators (MSO) would sign multi-year contracts with networks that specified the fee the network would receive for each household that received the channel. The local affiliates of that MSO marketed and distributed the service to consumers in all the local markets for which they held a franchise. For TFC, this negotiated subscriber fee averaged $1.00 per subscriber per year. The fee was paid entirely on the basis of carriage and did not go up or down as viewership changed. The TFC fee was at the low end of the industry range, reflecting the specialty niche content of the network. ESPN, and other networks that appealed to large numbers of households, charged the highest fees. Wheeler knew that the cable operators and affiliates carefully monitored customer satisfaction with network offerings and would threaten to drop unpopular channels. There were case studies of networks causing viewer outcry from unpopular changes. Consequently, it was important for TFC to maintain its general satisfaction level and keep the affiliates happy. Because TFC was widely distributed there was not much upside in affiliate revenue, though, and the general goal for both parties was to maintain a good equilibrium.

Wheeler closed the slide deck entirely. As far as cable affiliate revenue went, there wasn't much to be done, she thought. The network had already achieved virtually full penetration of available cable households and there was limited opportunity to raise fees. Wheeler knew that the two key levers to

---

[3] The formula for advertising revenue for an individual spot = (Households x Ratings)/1,000 x CPM.

---

drive revenue growth would be (1) increased viewership (ratings), and (2) increased advertising pricing.

She pulled out a legal pad and wrote: "Deliver quality audiences, as demanded by advertisers" across the top in large print.

Competitive Threats

The phone rang, breaking her concentration. "Dana," boomed Norm Frazier. "I'm running to a client meeting but just wanted to connect with you. I wanted to say, in the meeting next week, I hope we'll be able to talk about how to pitch TFC against the new fashion content on CNN and Lifetime. Lifetime is taking away a lot of ad buys from me because they're attracting younger female demographics. CNN is starting to deliver some great numbers on men. Both of these segments can be sold for a premium CPM, so we need to do something to draw these viewer groups back. If you want to talk before the meeting, just let me know."

Wheeler shook her head, understanding his impatience, but frustrated just the same. Still, this might be an opportunity to build consensus. "I'm on it, Norm. And thank you for the offer. I might take you up on it. My goal is to be able to come out of next week's meeting ready to take action immediately." They hung up, and Wheeler turned once again to her notepad, jotting down key points about the competitive landscape.

She picked up a folder and pulled out a summary of a recent Alpha research study on customer satisfaction with cable networks. The study showed that TFC was facing additional competitive challenges in its attractiveness to cable affiliates. On a scale of 1 to 5 (with 5 being the highest possible score), TFC had achieved a 3.8 rating on consumer interest in viewing, while the two competitors with new fashion programming had scored higher: CNN had scored 4.3 and Lifetime a 4.5 On awareness, TFC had scored 4.1 while CNN scored 4.6 and Lifetime a 4.5. On perceived value TFC was at 3.7, CNN 4.1 and Lifetime 4.4. [4] Cable operators used these data to determine how much to pay for each network, and also where they would include the network in their consumer offerings. The cable operator needed to offer service packages (often called tiers) that would appeal to the home consumer and would justify the monthly cable fee. If a network underperformed the averages, it risked being offered in less appealing packages, which could mean it would be seen in fewer households.

While TFC had generally scored above the midpoint, these data suggested that it was lagging two key networks that were now offering competitive programming. To Wheeler this indicated a need for marketing initiatives to improve consumer interest, awareness, and perceived value. Change would upset some viewers who liked the network's current programs and probably some TFC employees as well, but change would have to come.

She thought back to her final interviews with Jared Thomas, before he had offered her the position at TFC. "TFC can win in the market if the channel builds its marketing programs around the right consumer segmentation," she had told him. "First, you have to identify the customer groups that are most worth the effort to pursue. You can use market research not only for demographic data but also to study consumer behavior and attitudes—how viewers use the network, what they value, and what needs they have.

---

[4] The research had been conducted as a telephone survey of 800 U.S. cable households, who were all able to view all the networks. Households had been asked to rank the networks on a scale of 1-5 with 5 being the highest possible score: *Respondents were asked to rank on a scale of 1-5 (5= Most/Very/High; 4= Somewhat; 3 =Neutral/neither high nor low; 2= Not much; 1= Lowest/not at all).*

"It's likely that there's a core group willing to become very loyal to our network. These viewers have an emotional connection to TFC. We can find them and market to them so that we have the building blocks to create the brand loyalty that is hard for a competitor to take away."

Thomas had agreed, but confessed to being worried about viewers' fickleness. "It's easy to spend a fortune pursuing viewers who won't stay with you," he had cautioned. "There's an obvious risk in targeting only some of our customers. Some viewers could quit watching us and our ratings would decline."

She wondered what the management team would say when she presented her research and recommendations. They'd been at the network for several years and been buoyed by the growth that had been achieved with the something-for-everyone strategy. She expected there would be concern about doing anything that put revenue at risk, even in the short term.

Attitudinal Research Findings

Wheeler flipped open another folder on her desk to review the most recent consumer research reports that she'd commissioned. She removed two documents, which contained the highlights of a national consumer field study that had been completed in the previous month (**Exhibit 2**) by GFE Associates, a well-regarded market research firm. The researchers had asked a national panel of consumers more than 100 questions about their attitudes toward fashion and TFC as a way to understand the needs that the network served.

Attached to the data highlights was a second document (**Exhibit 3**) which GFE Associates had prepared compiling the results into attitudinal clusters. To create these clusters they had run the answers to all 100 questions through a sophisticated statistical correlation program to analyze patterns in the way consumers had answered. GFE Associates then constructed profiles for clusters of consumers who had common attitudes and needs. The report suggested four unique groups of viewers: Fashionistas, Planners & Shoppers, Situationalists, and Basics. While the segments varied in size, Wheeler quickly noticed that the smallest—the Fashionistas—had a high degree of interest in fashion. Wheeler also perceived several possible multi-cluster schemes, each of which would need to be judged according to

- How the scheme would impact the quantity of viewers (ratings);

- What the CPM advertising revenue potential would be;

- How TFC could be differentiated from current and future competition.

Most of the male interest occurred in the Basics cluster—the least likely to be engaged with TFC content. Wheeler had already concluded that it would be unwise to pursue additional male viewers only. Instead, she felt, TFC segmentation and positioning should be targeted at women, particularly the premium 18-to-34 year-old demographic.

She turned to a summary of the research on women. Since there were women aged 18 to 34 in all of the clusters, Wheeler first considered maintaining a broad appeal to a cross segment of Fashionistas, Planners & Shoppers, and Situationalists. By investing in a major marketing and advertising campaign as well as programming, it would be reasonable to expect that awareness and viewing of the channel would go up and could, over time, deliver a ratings boost of 20% (from the current 1.0 to 1.2). However, Ad Sales was forecasting a 10% drop in CPM to $1.80 if the current audience mix stayed the same – and a broad multi-cluster strategy might not deliver an audience different enough to avoid that fate. And there was always the risk that the competition would continue to penetrate the premium segments and further erode TFC's pricing ability.

An alternative to a broad, multi-segment approach would be to focus more on the Fashionistas. This segment was strong in the highly valued 18-34 female demographic. It was smaller than the other segments, representing only 15% of households, and so targeting them might lead to a drop in viewers—but it would also strengthen the value of the audience to advertisers, with a likely increase in CPM. Wheeler estimated that this strategy could deliver a rating of 0.8. Ad Sales had given her a projection of a $3.50 CPM for an audience stronger in the younger, female-oriented Fashionista segment. In addition to targeting this segment in marketing programs, Wheeler expected that it would be necessary to invest in new programming to attract and retain the interest of this segment. She estimated that she would need to spend an additional $15 million per year on programming under this scenario.

Wheeler was also interested in a third alternative scenario that targeted two segments—the Fashionistas and the Shoppers/Planners. She estimated that a dual targeting would drive average ratings over time to 1.2 with a potential CPM of $2.50. For this scenario she would need to spend an additional $20 million on programming to ensure that there were selections aimed at both segments.

Wheeler knew that her recommendation would have to show how her plan would increase TFC revenue and also quantify risks if the plan disappointed. She had created a revenue calculator spreadsheet to calculate the impact of ratings and CPM increases on potential TFC ad revenues (**Exhibit 4**). Now she opened up a new worksheet and prepared to look at the financial impact of these choices (see **Exhibit 5** for TFC 2006 and 2007 estimated financial statements). She would need to be prepared for many questions from Thomas and the other members of the leadership team. While everyone was aware of the changing competitive landscape, they really had not yet faced a decision about making real changes in order to stay ahead. Dana expected a vigorous discussion.

32

Exhibit 1 Viewer Demographics and Competitor Comparison (% Viewers; Adults over 18 years of age)

	All TV Viewers	The Fashion Channel	Lifetime: Fashion Today	CNN: Fashion Tonight
Time Period	24 x 7	24 x 7	M-F, 9-11 pm	M-F, 8-9 pm Sat.-Sun, 10-11 pm
Male	49%	39%	37%	45%
Female	51%	61%	63%	55%
18-34	30%	33%	43%	27%
35-54	41%	45%	42%	40%
54-74	21%	20%	14%	26%
>74	08%	02%	01%	02%
Income over $100,000	16%	18%	19%	17%
Average rating	NA	1.0	3.0	4.0
Average Households	110M	1.1M	3.3M	4.4M
Programming profile	All	Fashion news, features, and information	Fashion news and information	Fashion news and features with celebrity focus available

(References: US Census, business documents, casewriter estimates)

Rating - % TV households watching on average during measured viewing period.

Total TV households = 110 million

Exhibit 2 GFE Associates: National Consumer Survey (Excerpts)

Sample results from panel survey of consumers (% responding). Consumers were all cable subscribers and were selected to match the general demographic profile of this population.

	Strongly agree	Agree	Somewhat agree	Somewhat disagree	Disagree	Strongly disagree
1. It is important to me to know the most up to date fashion trends	16%	20%	19%	20%	15%	10%
2. I rely on television reports on fashion to plan what I will wear to work	6	11	20	25	18	20
3. I rely on television reports on fashion to plan what I will wear on special occasions	10	20	25	25	15	5
4. I like to watch special tv programs on current fashion	15	20	30	15	15	5
5. TFC is my favorite channel on cable	15	10	20	16	16	23
6. Shopping for new clothes is one of my favorite leisure activities	15	20	25	10	15	15
7. I like to shop for clothes for parties and special activities	20	21	20	15	10	14
8. I don't really enjoy shopping for clothes and only do it when necessary	15	15	21	20	15	14
9. I don't need information on fashion, I just wear what feels comfortable	20	15	20	15	15	15
10. I use fashion information to be sure my family is well dressed for special occasions	10	15	23	22	20	10
11. I like to know what people are wearing in other parts of the country	15	10	20	15	20	20
12. Fashion is more interesting than many things on television	15	12	15	24	19	15
13. I am willing to spend money on special clothes for special occasions	15	20	20	20	15	10
14. I shop around to find the best value on clothes	14	25	20	20	15	6
15. I like to talk to my friends and family about fashion	20	10	14	25	11	20
17. I participate in hobbies and sports that require special apparel	20	15	20	19	15	11
18. I like to plan what to wear in advance of work days and special events	15	20	10	20	20	15
19. I am more interested in fashion than most people	20	24	15	11	15	15
20. Watching fashion programs on television is very entertaining	25	20	10	10	20	15
21. TFC is the best place on television for fashion information	9%	21%	28%	20%	12%	10%

Exhibit 3 GFE Associates: Analysis of Attitudinal Clusters in U.S. Television Households for The Fashion Channel

Cluster	Involvement in Fashion	Size of Cluster (% HH)	Index: Interest in Fashion on TV (100=All viewer average)	Demographic Highlights	Attitude Drivers
Fashionistas	Highly engaged in fashion	15%	140	Female, 61% Income > $100k, 30% 18-34, 50%	Anticipate trends Stay up to date Think a lot about fashion Enjoy shopping Develop fashion expertise to share Fashion is entertaining
Planners & Shoppers	Participate in fashion on a regular basis	35%	110	Female, 53% 18-34, 25%	Stay up to date Enjoy shopping Fashion is practical Interested in value
Situationalists	Participate in fashion for specific needs	30%	105	Female, 50% Children in HH, 45% 18-34, 30%	Enjoy shopping for specific needs Think about fashion for specific situations Fashion is both entertaining and practical Interested in value
Basics	Disengaged	20%	50	Female, 45% Male, 55%	Do not enjoy shopping Do not spend much time thinking about what to wear Interested in value

> Index = Measure of segment interest in Fashion-oriented television vs. overall household interest in fashion television

Exhibit 4 Ad Revenue Calculator

NOTE: **Exhibits 4** and **5** are provided as a single Excel file to facilitate these calculations. To retrieve this file go to the HBS Publishing site (www.harvardbusinessonline.com) and search for this case exhibit product using product # 2278. Alternatively students may use the information presented in the case along with a calculator to manually fill in the blanks (shaded cells shown in the exhibit below).

Ad Revenue Calculator	Current	2007 Base	Scenario 1	Scenario 2	Scenario 3
TV HH	110,000,000	110,000,000	110,000,000	110,000,000	110,000,000
Average Rating	1.0%		*1.2*	*0.8*	*1.21*
Average Viewers (thousand)	1,100		*1320*	*880*	*1320*
Average CPM[a]	$2.00		*1.80*	*3.50*	*2.50*
Average Revenue/ Ad Minute[b]	$2,200	$0	*2376* $0	*3080* $0	*3300* $0
Ad Minutes/Week	2,016	2,016	2,016	2,016	2,016
Weeks/Year	52	52	52	52	52
Ad Revenue/Year	$230,630,400	$0	$0	$0	$0
Incremental Programming Expense				*15 mill*	*18 mill*

[a] Revenue/Thousand Viewers

[b] Calculated by multiplying Average Viewers by Average CPM

249,080,053

322,xxx,560

345,945,605

Exhibit 5 TFC Estimated Financials for 2006 and 2007.

NOTE: **Exhibits 4** and **5** are provided as a single Excel file to facilitate these calculations. To retrieve this file go to the HBS Publishing site (www.harvardbusinessonline.com) and search for this case exhibit product using product # 2278. Alternatively students may use the information presented in the case along with a calculator to manually fill in the blanks (shaded cells shown in the exhibit below).

	2006 Actual	2007 Base	Scenario 1	Scenario 2	Scenario 3	Assumptions
Revenue						
Ad Sales	$230,630,400		245,082,112	322,882,560	345,945,600	Insert scenario results from revenue calculator
Affiliate Fees	$80,000,000	$81,600,000	$81,600,000	$81,600,000	$81,600,000	Grows 2% per year with population
Total Revenue	$310,630,400	$81,600,000	$81,600,000	$81,600,000	$81,600,000	
			330680630	404,482560	427545600	
Expenses						
Cost of Operations	$70,000,000	$72,100,000	$72,100,000	$72,100,000	$72,100,000	Grows 3% per year with inflation
Cost of Programming	$55,000,000			15000000	20000000	Add incremental programming expense
Ad Sales Commissions	$6,918,912					3% of ad sales revenue
Marketing & Advertising	$45,000,000					Reflects increased spending of $15M
SGA	$40,000,000	$41,200,000	$41,200,000	$41,200,000	$41,200,000	Growing with inflation 3%
Total Expense	$216,918,912	$113,300,000	$113,300,000	$113,300,000	$113,300,000	Spreadsheet calculates automatically
Net Income	$93,711,488	2	217380015	89118260	314215600	Spreadsheet calculates automatically
Margin	30%					Spreadsheet calculates automatically

ROGER HALLOWELL

DAVID BOWEN

CARIN-ISABEL KNOOP

Four Seasons Goes to Paris: "53 Properties, 24 Countries, 1 Philosophy"

Europe is different from North America, and Paris is very different. I did not say difficult. I said different.

— A senior Four Seasons manager

In 2002, Four Seasons Hotels and Resorts was arguably the world's leading operator of luxury hotels, managing 53 properties in 24 countries and delivering what observers called "consistently exceptional service." For Four Seasons, that meant providing high-quality, truly personalized service to enable guests to *maximize the value of their time*, however the guest defined doing so.

In 1999, Four Seasons opened the Four Seasons Hotel George V Paris (hereafter, "F. S. George V"), its first French property, by renovating and operating the Hotel George V, a historic Parisian landmark. Doing so was, according to John Young, executive vice president, human resources, "one of our great challenges and triumphs." Young mused on what Four Seasons had learned from opening a hotel in France, wondering what lessons would be applicable to other openings given the firm's growth plans, which suggested that new opportunities would be largely outside North America. (**Exhibit 1** illustrates property locations in 2002.)

Performance

Four Seasons generally operated (as opposed to owned) midsized luxury hotels and resorts. From 1996 through 2000 (inclusive), Four Seasons revenues increased at a compound rate of 22.6% per year. Operating margins increased from 58.8% to 67.9% during the same period. Four Seasons' 2001 revenue per room (RevPAR) was 32% higher than that of its primary U.S. competitors and 27% higher than that of its European competitors. (**Exhibit 2** provides summary financials.)

Management Structure and Team

Structure   A general manager responsible for supervising the day-to-day operations of a single property oversaw each Four Seasons property. General managers had a target bonus of 30% of base compensation. A quarter of the bonus was based on people measures (employee attitudes), 25% on product (service quality), and 50% on property profit. Four Seasons management believed that the firm's regional management structure was "a key component" of its ability to deliver and maintain the highest and most consistent service standards at each property in a cost-effective manner. **Exhibit 3** describes this structure.

Italian in Italy, French in France   The firm's top managers were comfortable in a variety of international settings. Antoine Corinthios, president, Europe, Middle East, and Africa, for example, was said to be "Italian in Italy, French in France." Born and educated in Cairo, Corinthios spent 20 years in Chicago, but described himself as a world citizen. He was the cultural chameleon he wanted Four Seasons hotels to be. "If you are going global you cannot be one way," he explained.

No bragging, no excuses   Modesty, compassion, and discipline were also important. A manager who stayed on with Four Seasons described the Four Seasons due diligence team that came to the property as "very professional and not pretentious; detail oriented; and interested in people. They did not come telling me that all I did was wrong," he remembered, "and showed a lot of compassion." Excuses were not tolerated at Four Seasons: "Oh, but we have just been open a year" or "The people here do not understand" were not acceptable statements. Customer service extended to all levels in the organization: managers routinely helped clear restaurant tables in passing.

Strong allegiance to the firm   Four Seasons' top management team was noted for its longevity, many having been at the firm for over 25 years. Both corporate and field managers often referred to the firm as a "family," complete with rules, traditions, and tough love. There was a strong "one firm sentiment." For example, as one general manager explained, "We are happy to let stars go to other properties to help them."

Four Seasons' Approach to International Growth

Today, we have opened enough properties overseas that we can go into any city or town and pull people together to fulfill our mission.

— Isadore Sharp, founder and CEO

Diversity and Singularity

According to Corinthios, "Our strength is our diversity and our singularity. While the essence of the local culture may vary, the process for opening and operating a hotel is the same everywhere." He continued:

My goal is to provide an international hotel to the business or luxury leisure traveler looking for comfort and service. The trick is to take it a couple of notches up, or sideways, to adapt to the market you are in. Our standards are universal, for example, getting your message on time, clean room, good breakfast; being cared for by an engaging, anticipating, and responding staff; being able to treat yourself to an exciting and innovative meal—these are global. This is the fundamental value. What changes is that people do it with their own style, grace, and personality; in some cultures you add the strong local temperament. For example, an Italian concierge has his own style and flair. In Turkey or Egypt you experience different hospitality.

As a result, "each hotel is tailor made" and adapted to its national environment, noted David Crowl, vice president sales and marketing, Europe, Middle East, and Africa:

> Sharp once told me that one of our key strengths is diversity. McDonald's is the same all over. We do not want to be that way. We are not a cookie-cutter company. We try to make each property represent its location. In the rooms, we have 40 to 50 square meters to create a cultural destination without being offensive. When you wake up in our Istanbul hotel, you know that you are in Turkey. People know that they will get 24-hour room service, a custom-made mattress, and a marble bathroom, but they also know that they are going to be part of a local community.

David Richey, president of Richey International, a firm hired by Four Seasons and other hotel chains to audit service quality, believed that "Four Seasons has done an exceptional job adapting to local markets. From a design perspective they are much more clever than other companies. When you sit in the Four Seasons in Bali, you feel that you are in Bali. It does not scream 'Four Seasons' at you."

A manager explained Four Seasons' ability to be somewhat of a cultural chameleon with an analogy to Disney: "Unlike Disney, whose brand name is so strongly associated with the United States, Four Seasons' brand doesn't rigidly define what the product is. The Four Seasons brand is associated with intangibles. Our guests are not looking to stay in a Canadian hotel." In general, Four Seasons managers were wary of being perceived as an "American" company. They found it useful in Europe to position Four Seasons as the Canadian company it was.

According to Crowl, Four Seasons learned from each country and property: "Because we are an international hotel company, we take our learning across borders. At our new property in Egypt, we are going to try to incorporate indigenous elements to the spa, but we will still be influenced by the best practices we have identified at our two spas in Bali."

Globally Uniform Standards

The seven Four Seasons "service culture standards" expected of *all* staff *all* over the world at *all* times are described in **Exhibit 4**. In addition, Four Seasons had 270 core worldwide operating standards (see **Exhibit 5** for sample standards). Arriving at these standards had not been easy: until 1998 there were 800. With the firm's international growth, this resulted in an overly complex set of rules and exceptions. The standards were set by the firm's senior vice presidents and Wolf Hengst, president, Worldwide Hotel Operations, who explained: "We had a rule about the number of different types of bread rolls to be served at dinner and number of varieties of wine to be offered at lounges. In countries where no bread is eaten at dinner and no wine consumed, that's pretty stupid."

Exceptions to the 270 standards were permitted if they made local sense. For example, one standard stated that the coffee pot should be left on the table at breakfast so that guests could choose to refill their cup. This was perceived as a lack of service in France, so it was amended there. Standards were often written to allow local flexibility. While the standards required an employee's uniform to be immaculate, they did not state what it should look like. In Bali, uniforms were completely different from uniforms in Chicago. Managers emphasized that standards set *minimum expectations*: "If you can do something for a client that goes beyond a standard," they told staff, "do it." As a result, stories about a concierge bringing a client to the hospital and staying with that person overnight were part of Four Seasons lore.

3

To evaluate each property's performance against the standards, Four Seasons used both external and internal auditors. "Our standards are the foundation for all our properties," a senior manager noted. "It is the base on which we build." "When you talk to a Four Seasons person," Richey concluded, "they are so familiar with each of the standards, it is astonishing. With many managers at other firms, this isn't the case."

"We have been obsessed by the service standards," Hengst noted. "People who come from the outside are surprised that we take them and the role they play in our culture so seriously. But they are essential: talk to me about standards and you talk to me about religion." Another manager added, "Over time, the standards help to shape relationships between people, and those relationships contribute to building our culture."

Delivering "Intelligent, Anticipatory, and Enthusiastic Service" Worldwide

A manager stated: "We decided many years ago that our distinguishing edge would be exceptional, personal service—that's where the value is. In all our research around the world, we have never seen anything that led us to believe that 'just for you' customized service was not the most important element of our success." Another manager added, "Service like this—what I think of as 'intelligent service'—can't be scripted. As a result, we need employees who are as distinguished as our guests. If employees are going to adapt, to be empathetic and anticipate guest needs, the 'distance' between the employee and the guest has to be small."

There were also tangible elements to Four Seasons' service quality. The product was always comfortable—so much so that at guests' requests, the company made its pillows, bedspreads, and mattresses available for sale. "However, there are differences in the perception and definition of luxury," explained Barbara Talbott, executive vice president of marketing. "In the United States, our properties have public spaces with a luxurious, but intimate, feeling. In the Far East, our properties have large lobbies enabling guests to see and be seen. People around the world also have different ways of using a hotel—restaurants, for example, are more important in hotels in Asia, so we build space for more restaurants in each property there."

Human Resources and "The Golden Rule"

Human resource management at Four Seasons started and ended with "The Golden Rule," which stipulated that one should treat others as one would wish to be treated. "The Golden Rule is the key to the success of the firm," founder and CEO Sharp emphasized, "and it's appreciated in every village, town, and city around the world. Basic human needs are the same everywhere." Kathleen Taylor, president, Worldwide Business Operations, provided an example of how Four Seasons implemented the Golden Rule: "We give employees several uniforms so they can change when they became dirty. That goes to their dignity, but it is uncommon in the hospitality industry. People around the world want to be treated with dignity and respect, and in most organizational cultures that doesn't happen." (**Exhibit 6** summarizes the firm's goals, beliefs, and principles.)

Managers acknowledged that many service organizations made similar statements on paper. They believed that what differentiated Four Seasons was how the chain operationalized those statements. Crowl noted: "A service culture is about putting what we all believe in into practice. We learn it, we nurture it, and most important, we do it." "People make the strength of this company," a senior manager stated. "Procedures are not very varied or special. What we do is fairly basic."

4

In 2002, for the fifth year in a row, Four Seasons was on *Fortune* magazine's list of the top 100 best companies to work for in North America. Four Seasons' turnover was half that of the hospitality industry average of 55%.

Going to Paris

Despite the success of Four Seasons' approach and philosophy, management knew that entering France would be a challenge.

The George V Opportunity

The six hotels in Paris classified as "Palaces" were grand, historic, and luxurious. Standard room prices at the F. S. George V, for example, ranged from $400 to $700. Most palaces featured award-winning restaurants, private gardens, and expansive common areas. The nine-story George V was designed in the 1920s by two famous French art déco architects. (**Exhibit 7** provides comparative data on Parisian palaces.)

Observers of the Paris hotel scene noted that by the 1980s and 1990s, the George V, like some of its peers, was coasting on its reputation. In December 1996, H.R.H. Prince Al Waleed Bin Talal Bin Abdulaziz al Saud purchased the hotel for $170 million. In November 1997, Four Seasons agreed to manage the hotel. "We needed to be in Paris," Young explained. "We had looked at a new development, but gaining planning permission for a new building in Paris is very hard. Since we look for the highest possible quality assets in the best locations, the George V was perfect. It established us very powerfully in the French capital."

Physical Renovations

Four Seasons' challenge was to preserve the soul of the legendary, almost mythical George V Hotel while rebuilding it for contemporary travelers. Four Seasons closed the hotel for what ended up being a two-year, $125 million total renovation. Since the building was a landmark, the façade had to be maintained. The interior of the hotel, however, was gutted. Skilled craftsmen restored the façade's art déco windows and balconies, extensive wood paneling, gilding, artwork, and 17th-century Flanders tapestries that had long adorned the hotel's public and private spaces.

The interior designer hired by Four Seasons, Pierre-Yves Rochon, noted: "I would like guests re-discovering the hotel to think that I had not changed a thing—and, at the same time, to notice how much better they feel within its walls."[1] The fact that the designer was French, Barbara Talbott pointed out, "signaled to the French that we understood what they meant by luxury."

While Four Seasons built to American safety standards, it also had to adhere to local laws, which affected design and work patterns. For example, a French hygiene law stipulated that food and trash be carried down different corridors and up and down different elevators. Another law involved the "right to light": employees had the right to work near a window for a certain number of hours each day. As a result, employees in the basement spa also worked upstairs in a shop with a window for several hours a day, and as many windows as possible had to be programmed into the design.

The new Four Seasons Hotel George V Paris opened on December 18, 1999, at 100% effective occupancy (occupancy of rooms ready for use). The opening was particularly challenging because Four Seasons only took formal control of operations on December 1, in part due to French regulations. "The French are very particular about, for example, fire regulations, but the fire department would not come in and inspect until everything else was complete," a manager said.

Becoming a French Employer

Entering the French hospitality market meant becoming a French employer, which implied understanding French labor laws, business culture, and national idiosyncrasies.

Rules

France's leaders maintained social equity with laws, tax policies, and social spending that reduced income disparity and the impact of free markets on public health and welfare.[2] France's tax burden, 45% of GDP in 1998, was 3% higher than the European average—and 8% higher than the OECD average. An additional burden on employers was the 1999 reduction of the workweek to 35 hours. Unemployment and retirement benefits were generous.

The country was also known for its strong unions.[3] A French manager pointed out, "In France, one still finds a certain dose of antagonism between employees and management." The political party of the union that was strongest at the F. S. George V garnered nearly 10% of votes in the first round of the 2002 French presidential election with the rallying cry, "Employees fight the bosses!"

Four Seasons management was not unfamiliar with labor-oriented government policy. Young explained that "Canada has many attributes of a welfare state, so our Canadian roots made it easier to deal with such a context." Corinthios added, "If you look at the challenges of operating in France, they have labor laws that are restrictive, but not prohibitive. The laws are not the same as, for example, in Chicago. You just need to be more informed about them." The laws did give employers some flexibility, allowing them to work someone a little more during peak business periods and less during a lull. A housekeeper, for example, might work 40-hour weeks in the summer in exchange for a few 30-hour weeks in the late fall. Furthermore, French employers could hire 10% to 15% of staff on a "temporary," seasonal basis.

A particularly tricky area of labor management in France involved terminations. "Wherever we operate in the world," a Four Seasons manager explained, "we do not fire at will. There is due process. There is no surprise. There is counseling. So, Paris isn't that different, except to have the termination stick is more challenging because you really need a very, *very* good cause and to document *everything* carefully. If you have one gap in the documentation, you will have to rehire the terminated employee."

National and Organizational Culture

Geert Hofstede's seminal work, *Culture's Consequences*,[4] indicated a great disparity between North American (U.S. and Canadian) national culture and that of France.[5] Four Seasons managers agreed; Corinthios identified attitudes on performance evaluation as one difference:

> European and Middle Eastern managers have a hard time sitting across from people they supervise and talking about their weaknesses. The culture is not confrontational. It is more congenial and positive. It is very important to save face and preserve the dignity of the person being reviewed. Some Four Seasons managers using standard forms might even delete certain sections or questions or reprogram them in different languages.

6

42

For Didier Le Calvez, general manager of the F. S. George V and recently appointed regional vice president, another significant difference was the degree to which middle and front-line managers felt accountable. "The greatest challenge in France is to get managers to take accountability for decisions and policies," he said. "In the French hierarchical system, there is a strong tendency to refer things to the boss."

Le Calvez was also surprised by managers' poor understanding of human resource issues. In France, when a manager had a problem with an employee, the issue generally was referred to the human resources department. "We, at Four Seasons, require that operating managers be present, deal with the issue, and lead the discussion."

Saint Thomas the Skeptic

When reflecting on their experiences with employees in France, several Four Seasons managers mentioned Saint Thomas ("doubting Thomas"). "They must see it to believe it," Le Calvez explained. "They do not take things at face value. They also tend to wait on the sidelines—once they see that something works, they come out of their shells and follow the movement." A Four Seasons manager continued:

> Most of the workforce in France did not know what Four Seasons was all about. For example, they did not think we were serious about the Golden Rule. They thought it was way too American. Initially, there were some eyebrows raised. Because of this skepticism, when we entered France, we came on our tiptoes, without wanting to give anyone a lecture. I think *how* we came in was almost as important as *what* we did.

More Differences

For several Four Seasons managers, working in France required a "bigger cultural adjustment" than had been necessary in other countries. "In France, I always knew that I would be a foreigner," a manager explained. "It took me a while to adjust to the French way." "There is simply an incredible pride in being French," added another. "The French have a very emotional way of doing things," an F. S. George V manager explained. "This can be good and bad. The good side is that they can be very joyous and engaging. On the bad side, sometimes the French temper lashes out."

According to Four Seasons managers, what was referred to in the cultural research literature as the French "logic of honor"[6] was strong. While it would be degrading to be "in the service of" (*au service de*) anybody, especially the boss, it was honorable to "give service" (*rendre service*), with magnanimity, if asked to do so with due ceremony. In this context, management required a great deal of tact and judgment.

Managing differing perceptions of time could also be a challenge for North Americans in France. North Americans have been characterized by cultural researchers as having a "monochronic" culture based on a high degree of scheduling and an elaborate code of behavior built around promptness in meeting obligations and appointments.[7] In contrast, the French were said to be "polychronic," valuing human relationships and interactions over arbitrary schedules and appointments. These differences created predictable patterns, summarized in **Exhibit 8**.

Cultural Renovation at the F.S. George V

Young noted:

> When we explored options for refashioning the George V into a Four Seasons hotel we realized that without being able to start from scratch, the task would be Herculean. The existing culture was inconsistent with ours. In a North American environment you can decide whom to keep after an acquisition at a cost you can determine in advance on the basis of case law. In France, the only certainty is that you cannot replace the employees. You are acquiring the entity as a going concern. Unless you do certain things, you simply inherit the employees, including their legal rights based on prior service.

To be able to reduce headcount, by law an enterprise had to plan to be closed for over 18 months. Because the F.S. George V owner wanted the renovation to be complete in 12 months, staff were guaranteed a position with Four Seasons unless they chose to leave.[8] "Many of the best employees easily found other jobs, while the most disruptive were still there when the hotel reopened," Young said. "The number of people we really didn't want was somewhere in the region of 40 out of 300 coming back on reopening."

Young provided an example of the cultural problems Four Seasons found: "During the due diligence process the former general manager went to lunch with one of our senior staff. Even though guests were waiting, the maitre d' immediately tried to escort the general manager and his party to the general manager's customary table. At Four Seasons this is seen as an abuse of privilege. For us, 'the guest always comes first.'"

Fortunately, in taking over The Pierre in New York in 1981, Four Seasons had been through a similar process. As a senior Four Seasons manager recalled, "Shortly after we bought The Pierre, a bell captain lamented that the times of the big steamer trunks were over. The staff had not adjusted to jet travel, despite its prevalence for two decades. This is the same kind of recalibration we had to do at the George V."

Apples and Oranges

The Four Seasons had developed a specific approach to cultural transformation in acquired properties with existing staffing. Young elaborated:

> If we can achieve a critical mass of individuals among the workforce committed to doing things differently, to meeting our standards, that critical mass overcomes the resistance of what becomes a diminishing old guard. Progressively, that old guard loses some of its power. If one rotten apple can ruin the barrel, then you have to seed the organization with oranges that cannot be spoiled by the apples. As a result, a departing old-guard employee is *very* carefully replaced. Concurrently, individuals with the right culture and attitude are promoted. That creates a new culture, bit by bit by bit. At the F. S. George V, we also appealed to the national pride of our staff to help us restore a French landmark—restore the pride of France.

"Un Boss Franco-Français"

To effect this cultural change, Four Seasons chose Le Calvez to be general manager. Described as both demanding and "Franco-Français,"[9] an expression describing someone or something "unequivocally French," Le Calvez brought extensive Four Seasons and North American experience.

Prior to opening the Regent Hotel in Singapore, he had spent 25 years outside France, including 11 years at The Pierre in New York.

Young commented on the choice of Le Calvez: "The choice of senior leadership is absolutely critical. Adherence to our values and operational goals has to be extremely strong. Hotel openings require a lot of patience and tolerance because results are likely to be less positive as you manage through periods of major change."

"The hotel's culture is embodied in the general manager," an F.S. George V manager noted. In a country where people typically referred to each other as Monsieur and Madame with their last name, Le Calvez encouraged the use of the first name. "It is more direct, relaxed, and straightforward. It represents the kind of relationship I want to have with my staff," he stated.

The Task Force

To help Le Calvez and his team "Four Seasonize" the F. S. George V staff and ensure a smooth opening, Four Seasons assigned a 35-person task force, as it did for every new property. The task force, composed of experienced Four Seasons managers and staff, reflected the operating needs of each property. For example, if an experienced room service manager had already transferred to the opening property, those skills would not be brought in via the task force. A manager noted:

> The task force helps establish norms and helps people understand how Four Seasons does things. Members listen for problems and innuendoes, communicate the right information to all, and squash rumors, especially when there are cultural sensitivities. The task force also helps physically getting the property up and running. Finally, being part of the task force exposes managers—who may one day become general managers—to the process of opening a hotel.

"The task force is truly a human resource, as well as strong symbol," a manager explained. "The approach supports allegiance to the firm and not just one property." Most task force members, who typically stayed three weeks for an opening, stayed seven to eight weeks at the F. S. George V.

Strong Tides

After working 25 years abroad, Le Calvez admitted that he was hesitant to return to work in France in light of the tension he sensed between labor and management. However, he was encouraged by what he had seen at The Pierre, where Four Seasons managers noted that they had fostered a dialogue with the New York hospitality industry union. Le Calvez felt he could do the same in Paris: "When I arrived I told the unions that I did not think that we would need them, but since the law said we had to have them, I said 'let's work together.' I do not want social tensions. Of course, this is not unique to me, it is Four Seasons' approach. We have to be pragmatic. So we signaled our commitment to a good environment."

Le Calvez communicated this commitment by openly discussing the 35-hour workweek, the Four Seasons retirement plan, and the time and attendance system, designed to make sure that staff would not work more than required. At the outset of negotiations, in preparation for the reopening, Le Calvez took the representatives of the various unions to lunch. As work progressed, he organized tours of the site so that representatives could see what was being done and "become excited" about the hotel. Managers stated that the unions were not accustomed to such an inclusive approach in France.

Young felt that dealing with unions in France was easier than in New York: "In France, you are dealing with an institution backed by stringent, but predictable, laws. In the United States, you are dealing with individuals in leadership who can be much more volatile and egocentric."

Young referred, again, to the Four Seasons experience with The Pierre:

> In New York, we redesigned working spaces, and trained, and trained, and trained staff. But we also burned out a couple of managers. The old culture either wears you down or you wear it down. In an environment with strong labor laws, management sometimes gives up the right to manage. At some point managers stop swimming against the tide. If that continues long enough, the ability to manage effectively is lost. The precedents in a hotel are those that the prior managers have permitted. If the right to manage has been given up, standards are depressed, productivity and margins decrease, and eventually you have a bad business. Regulars are treated well, but many guests are not. Reversing this process requires enormous management energy. It is very wearing to swim against a strong tide. You are making decisions that you believe reasonable and facing reactions that you believe unreasonable.

The 35-hour Workweek

Four Seasons managers implemented the 35-hour workweek at the F. S. George V in order to meet the letter and spirit of French law. "When we hire staff from other hotels they are always surprised that we obey the law," an F. S. George V manager noted. "They worked more elsewhere."

A 35-hour workweek yielded 1,820 workable hours per full-time staff equivalent. But since the French had more holidays and vacation, an employee provided 1,500 to 1,600 workable hours, compared with approximately 1,912 hours in the United States for a full-time equivalent. A manager commented, "We did not really understand the impact of the 35-hour workweek. Each of our 80 managers has to have two consecutive days off a week, and each of the staff can work 214 days a year. Not 215. Not 213. But 214."

In 2002, 620 staff covered 250 rooms, or 2.5 staff per room. On average, Four Seasons hotels had 1.6 employees per room. Depending on food and banquet operations, that average could rise or fall significantly. (**Exhibit 9** shows employees-to-room ratios at selected Four Seasons properties.) Young felt that, compared with U.S. norms, labor laws explained about 15% of the need for increased staff ratios in Paris; vacations and holidays, 10%; with the balance explained by other factors including logistics of the operation, e.g., a historic building. Corinthios elaborated:

> In Paris, six palaces compete for the same clients. It is a more formal operation. Guest expectations are very high, as is the level of leisure business (which requires higher staffing). People stay four to six days and use the concierge extensively. The concierge staffing at the F. S. George V is as big as anything we have in the chain. Then there is more emphasis on food and beverage. We have a fabulous chef and more staff in the kitchen for both the restaurant and room service—expectations of service in the gastronomic restaurant are very high.

Running the F. S. George V

Recruitment and Selection

Four Seasons wanted to be recognized as the best employer in each of its locations. Salaries (which were among the top three for hotels) were advertised in help wanted ads, a first in the industry in Paris, according to F. S. George V managers.

At the F. S. George V, as across the firm, every potential employee was interviewed four times, the last interview being with the general manager. According to one executive, "In the selection process, we try to look deep inside the applicant. I learned about the importance of service from my parents—did this potential employee learn it from hers?" "What matters is attitude, attitude, attitude," Corinthios explained. "All around the world it is the same. Without the right attitude, they cannot adapt." Another manager added, "What we need is people who can adapt, either to guests from all over the world or to operating in a variety of countries." One of his colleagues elaborated on the importance of hiring for attitude, and its challenges:

> You would think that you would have a lot of people with great experience because there are so many palace hotels in Paris. But because we hire for attitude, we rarely hire from the other palaces. We hire individuals who are still "open" and tend to be much younger than usual for palace hotels. Then we bet on training. Of course, it takes much longer to train for skills when people do not have them. We look for people persons, who are welcoming and put others at ease, who want to please, are professional and sincerely friendly, flexible, smiley, and positive. At the F. S. George V people apply for jobs because they have friends who work here.

To spread the culture and "de-demonize" the United States, the new F. S. George V management recruited staff with prior Four Seasons and/or U.S. experience to serve as ambassadors. A manager noted, "Staff with U.S. experience share with other staff what the United States is about and that it is not the terrible place some French people make it out to be." About 40 individuals had prior North American and international experience.

"Anglo-Saxon" Recognition, Measurement, and Benefits

Le Calvez and his team launched an employee-of-the-month and employee-of-the-year program. "This had been controversial at Disney. People said it could not be done in France, but we managed to do it quite successfully. It all depends how it is presented," Le Calvez noted. "We explained that it would recognize those who perform. Colleagues can tell who is good at their job."

Le Calvez used the same spirit to introduce annual evaluations, uncommon in France:

> People said it would be unpopular, but the system seems to work. We told the staff that it would be an opportunity for open and constructive dialogue so that employees can know at all times where they stand. This allows them to adapt when need be. We made clear that there would be no favoritism, but rather that this would be a meritocracy. Here your work speaks for itself. The idea that your work is what matters could be construed as very Anglo Saxon!

Implementing the "Golden Rule"

F. S. George V's human resource director commented: "Cooks, before joining Four Seasons, used to have very long days, starting in the morning to prepare for lunch, having a break during the afternoon, and coming back to prepare dinner. Today, they work either a morning or afternoon shift, enabling a better organization of their personal lives."

"All these gestures take time to work," Le Calvez summarized. "At first, employees do not think we mean it. Some new hires think it's artificial or fake, but after a few months they let their guard down when they realize we mean what we say."

Managers believed that the effect of Four Seasons' human resource practices was reflected in customer satisfaction. Le Calvez noted, "We offer friendly, very personal service. We have a very young and dynamic brigade with an average age of 26, spanning 46 different nationalities."

Communication

To promote communication and problem solving, the F. S. George V management implemented a "direct line": once a month the general manager met with employees, supervisors, and managers in groups of 30 (employees met separately from supervisors—because subordinates in France did not feel comfortable speaking up in front of superiors). The groups met for three consecutive months so that issues raised could be addressed, with results reported to the group. Managers believed that the F. S. George V was the only palace hotel in France with such a communication process.

Every morning the top management team gathered to go over glitches—things that may have gone wrong the day before and the steps that had been, or were being taken, to address the problem. "Admitting what went wrong is not in the French culture," a French Four Seasons manager explained. "But the meetings are usually very constructive."

Finally, about three times a year, Le Calvez and his team hosted an open door event inviting employees and their families to spend time at the hotel. "This is to break down barriers," he explained. "We take people around the hotel, into the back corridors. Try to remind people of a notion that is unfortunately being lost—that of the *plaisir du travail*—or enjoying one's work. Furthermore, we celebrate achievement. Good property rankings, for example, are recognized with special team celebrations."

The property also cultivated external communication with the press in a way that was culturally sensitive. Le Calvez and his team felt that they had been very open and responsive to the press (which they stated was unusual in France) and that as a result "not a single negative article had been written about Four Seasons Hotel George V since its opening." A colleague added, "The press appreciated they were dealing with locals: it was not like Disney where everyone was American."

Culinary Coup d'Etat

In a diversion from Four Seasons practice, a non-Four Seasons executive chef was hired, Philippe Legendre, from the world-famous Parisian restaurant Taillevent. "In France, having a serious chef and serious food is important," noted the F.S. George V assistant food and beverage director. "You cannot be a palace hotel without that."

"Didier [Le Calvez] came to get me through a common friend," Legendre explained. Legendre said he accepted Four Seasons' offer because "there was something exciting about being part of opening a hotel. " He also liked Four Seasons' language, which he described as "optimistic" and "about creating possibilities." Legendre felt that Four Seasons' real strength was around guest and employee relationship management, which "is not something that we are that good at in France, or place particular emphasis on. We have a lot to learn in the social domain. Everything at Four Seasons is geared towards the needs of the guest. At first it was hard, especially the training. Perhaps because in France, we think we know everything." He continued: "After three years, I might not talk the Four Seasons talk, I might not use the same words, but I have the same view and adhere to the same system."

Despite Legendre's success (earning two Michelin stars), a colleague added, "Bringing in such an executive chef was problematic. The challenge is that with this chef you have someone with extraordinary talent, but who must still adjust to the way service is delivered at Four Seasons." Legendre described a situation illustrating miscommunication and cultural differences, which required tremendous patience on the part of the restaurant, guests, and management:

> Recently a man ordered an omelet and his wife ordered scrambled eggs. The man returned the omelet because he decided he wanted scrambled eggs. We made them. Then he sent them back because they did not meet his expectations. Of course, we realize that our *oeufs brouillés* are different from scrambled eggs, which don't contain cream. Because we are Four Seasons we cooked the eggs as he wanted them, like American scrambled eggs, and didn't charge for them. But cooking is about emotion—if you want to please someone, you have to do it with your heart. *We live differently in France.*

Results: A Cultural Cocktail

The F. S. George V was, in effect, a cultural cocktail. Le Calvez explained, "The F. S. George V is not *only* a French hotel—it is French, but it is also very international. We want to be different from the other palaces that are oh so very French. We want to project the image of a modern France, one that does not have to be dusty. We want to be a symbol of a France that is in movement, a European France, a France that stands for integration and equality."

The cultural cocktail also contained some elements that were unusual in France. At the time of the opening, journalists asked about the "American" smiling culture, which was referred to in France as "la culture Mickey Mouse." Le Calvez replied, "If you tell me that being American is being friendly and pleasant, that is fine by me. People tell me everyone smiles at the Four Seasons George V."

The spectacular flowers in the lobby of the F. S. George V (a single urn once contained 1,000 roses) were both very French and extremely international. "Paris is a city of fashion and culture, artistic and innovative," Le Calvez explained. "That is why, for example, we have the flowers we do. We can do that here." However, the flowers were designed by a young American. Another departure from French standard was the decision to hire women as concierges, and men in housekeeping. Managers viewed these decisions as revolutionary steps in Paris.

Service Quality

Richey summarized the results of the first F. S. George V service quality audit in October 2000:

This audit occurred less than one year after opening, and it takes at least a year to get things worked out. There were three things we talked to Four Seasons' executives about, mostly related to employee attitude. First, the staff had an inability to apologize or empathize. I think that could be construed as typically European, and especially French. Second, the team had a very tough time doing anything that could be described as selling. This is also typically European. For example: say your glass is empty at the bar. In Paris, they may not ask you if you want another drink. Third, the staff were rules and policy oriented. If something went wrong, they would refer to the manual instead of focusing on satisfying the guest.

Things had changed considerably by Richey's second audit in August 2001, when "they beat the competitive market set." The scores showed a significant improvement, raising the property to Four Seasons' system average.

More good news came in July 2002 with the results of an Employee Opinion Survey, in which 95% of employees participated. The survey yielded an overall rating of 4.02 out of 5. The statements that ranked the highest were: "I am proud to work for Four Seasons Hotels and Resorts" (4.65) and "I would want to work here again" (4.61).

The property also received several industry awards including Andrew Harper's Hideaway Report 2001 and 2002, World's Best Hotels and Resorts, Travel & Leisure Readers' Choice Awards 2001 #2 Best Hotel in Europe, and #5 World's Best Hotel Spa.

Exhibit 1   Overview of Property Locations

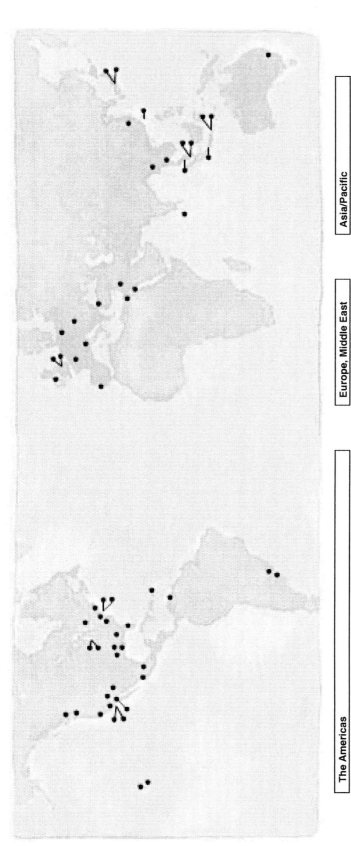

The Americas

Atlanta
Austin
Aviara, North San Diego
Boston
Buenos Aires
Caracas
Carmelo, Uruguay
Chicago
Chicago (The Ritz-Carlton)
Dallas
Hawaii
Houston
Las Vegas
Los Angeles
Los Angeles (the Regent Beverly Wilshire)

Maui
Nevis
New York
New York (The Pierre)
Newport Beach
Palm Beach
Philadelphia
Punta Mita, México
San Francisco
Santa Barbara
Scottsdale
Seattle
Toronto
Vancouver
Washington, D.C.

Europe, Middle East

Amman
Berlin
Cairo
Dublin
Istanbul
Lisbon
London
London, Canary Wharf
Milan
Paris
Prague
Sharm El Sheikh

Asia/Pacific

Bali at Jimbaran Bay
Bali at Sayan
Bangkok (The Regent)
Chiang Mail (The Regent)
Jakarta (The Regent)
Kuala Lumpur (The Regent)
Maldives
Shanghai
Singapore
Singapore (The Regent)
Sydney
Taipei (Grand Formosa Regent)
Tokyo at Chinzan-so
Tokyo at Marunouchi

Source: Four Seasons Web site, <http://www.fourseasons.com/find_a_hotel.html>.

Exhibit 2   Summary Financial Data

Consolidated Balance Sheets

(in thousands of dollars)	Years Ended December 31	
	2001	2000
ASSETS		
Current assets:		
Cash and cash equivalents	$210,421	$218,100
Receivables	78,450	94,265
Inventory	3,074	2,806
Prepaid expenses	2,492	1,499
	294,437	316,670
Long-term receivables	201,453	167,214
Investments in hotel partnerships and corporations	141,005	172,579
Fixed assets	50,715	46,342
Investment in management contracts	201,460	189,171
Investment in trademarks and trade names	33,784	34,829
Future income tax assets	17,745	21,771
Other assets	39,782	35,821
	$980,381	$984,397
LIABILITIES AND SHAREHOLDERS' EQUITY		
Current liabilities:		
Accounts payable and accrued liabilities	$ 50,813	$ 71,345
Long-term obligations due within one year	1,188	1,152
	52,001	72,497
Long-term obligations	118,244	203,736
Shareholders' equity:		
Capital stock	319,460	316,640
Convertible notes	178,543	178,543
Contributed surplus	4,784	4,784
Retained earnings	285,619	202,760
Equity adjustment from foreign currency translation	21,730	5,437
	$810,136	$708,164
Commitments and contingencies	$980,381	$984,397

Source: Four Seasons Web site, <http://www.fourseasons.com/investor/annual_reports/2001/cfs_cso.htm>.

Exhibit 2 (continued)

Consolidated Statement of Operations

(in thousands of dollars except per-share amounts)	Years Ended December 31	
	2001	2000
CONSOLIDATED REVENUES	$303,106	$347,507
Management Operations		
Revenues	$160,672	$185,294
General and administrative expenses	(65,416)	(59,532)
	95,256	125,762
Ownership Operations		
Revenues	147,500	161,061
Distributions from hotel investments	1,510	9,047
Expenses:		
Cost of sales and expenses	(152,663)	(148,590)
Fees to Management Operations	(6,576)	(7,895)
	(10,229)	13,623
Earnings before other operating items	85,027	139,385
Depreciation and amortization	(16,242)	(14,028)
Other income, net	30,698	8,669
Earnings from operations	99,483	134,026
Interest income, net	6,740	4,190
Earnings before income taxes	106,223	138,216
Income tax recovery (expense):		
Current	(15,711)	(33,412)
Future	(3,087)	1,796
Reduction of future income tax assets	(939)	(3,526)
	(19,737)	(35,142)
Net earnings	$ 86,486	$103,074
Earnings per share	$ 2.48	$ 2.98
Diluted earnings per share	$ 2.27	$ 2.63

Source: Four Seasons Web site, <http://www.fourseasons.com/investor/annual_reports/2001/cfs_cbs.htm>.

Exhibit 3   Four Seasons Reporting Structure

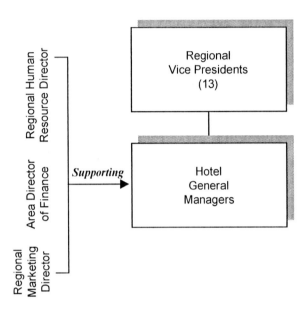

Source: Company data.

Notes: A general manager typically reported to a Regional Vice President (RVP) selected from the ranks of senior General Managers. The criteria for promotion to RVP included breadth of experience (various geographic locations; city/resort/opening hotels), business skills, and capability to represent the standards and culture of Four Seasons. Each RVP continued to operate as General Manager of his or her base hotel, while acting as the first recourse for advice, guidance, policy interpretation, people, product, and owner-relations issues. A region normally comprised the base hotel/resort plus two or three hotels within reasonable traveling distance of the RVP's base hotel.

Exhibit 4   The Seven Four Seasons "Service Culture Standards"

1.	**S**MILE	Employees will actively greet guests, SMILE, and speak clearly in a friendly manner.
2.	**E**YE	Employees will make EYE contact, even in passing, with an acknowledgment.
3.	**R**ECOGNITION	All staff will create a sense of RECOGNITION by using the guest's name, when known, in a natural and discreet manner.
4.	**V**OICE	Staff will speak to guests in an attentive, natural, and courteous manner, avoiding pretension, and in a clear VOICE.
5.	**I**NFORMED	All guest contact staff will be well INFORMED about their hotel and their product, will take ownership of simple requests, and will not refer guests elsewhere.
6.	**C**LEAN	Staff will always appear CLEAN, crisp, well groomed, and well fitted.
7.	**E**VERYONE	EVERYONE, everywhere, all the time, show their care for our guests.

Source: Company data.

Exhibit 5   Sample Core Standards

RESERVATIONS

Mission: To provide crisp, knowledgeable, and friendly service, sensitive to the guest's time and dedication to finding the most suitable accommodation.

- Phone service will be highly efficient, including: answered before the fourth ring; no hold longer than 15 seconds; or, in case of longer holds, call-backs offered, then provided in less than 3 minutes.

- After establishing the reason for the guest visit, reservationist automatically describes the guest room colorfully, attempting to have the guest picture himself or herself in the room.

HOTEL ARRIVAL

Mission: To make all guests feel welcome as they approach, and assured that details are well tended; to provide a speedy, discreet, and hassle-free arrival for business travelers; to provide a comforting and luxurious arrival for leisure travelers.

- The doorman (or first-contact employee) will actively greet guests, smile, make eye contact, and speak clearly in a friendly manner.

- The staff will be aware of arriving vehicles and will move toward them, opening doors within 30 seconds.

- Guests will be welcomed at the curbside with the words "welcome" and "Four Seasons" (or hotel name), and given directions to the reception desk.

- No guest will wait longer than 60 seconds in line at the reception desk.

MESSAGES AND PAGING

Mission: To make guests feel that their calls are important, urgent, and require complete accuracy.

- Phone service will be highly efficient, including: answered before the fourth ring; no longer than 15 seconds.

- Callers requesting guest room extensions between 1 a.m.–6 a.m. will be advised of the local time and offered the option of leaving a message or putting the call through.

- Unanswered guest room phones will be picked up within 5 rings, or 20 seconds.

- Guests will be offered the option of voice mail; they will not automatically be routed to voice mail OR they will have a clear option to return to the operator.

Exhibit 5 (continued)

GUEST ROOM EVENING SERVICE

Mission: To create a sense of maximum comfort and relaxation.   When meeting guests, to provide a sense of respect and discretion.

- Guest clothing that is on the bed or floor will be neatly folded and placed on the bed or chair; guest clothing left on other furniture will be neatly folded and left in place; shoes will be paired.

- Newspapers and periodicals will be neatly stacked and left on a table or table shelf in plain view; guest personal papers will not be disturbed in any way.

- Guest toiletries will be neatly arranged on a clean, flat cloth.

Source: Company data.

Exhibit 6   Four Seasons Goals, Beliefs, and Principles

Who We Are: We have chosen to specialize within the hospitality industry by offering only experiences of exceptional quality. Our objective is to be recognized as the company that manages the finest hotels, resorts, residence clubs, and other residential projects wherever we locate. We create properties of enduring value using superior design and finishes, and support them with a deeply instilled ethic of personal service. Doing so allows Four Seasons to satisfy the needs and tastes of our discriminating customers, to maintain our position as the world's premier luxury hospitality company.

What We Believe: Our greatest asset, and the key to our success, is our people. We believe that each of us needs a sense of dignity, pride, and satisfaction in what we do. Because satisfying our guests depends on the united efforts of many, we are most effective when we work together cooperatively, respecting each other's contribution and importance.

How We Behave: We demonstrate our beliefs most meaningfully in the way we treat each other and by the example we set for one another. In all our interactions with our guests, business associates, and colleagues, we seek to deal with others as we would have them deal with us.

How We Succeed: We succeed when every decision is based on a clear understanding of and belief in what we do and when we couple this conviction with sound financial planning. We expect to achieve a fair and reasonable profit to ensure the prosperity of the company, and to offer long-term benefits to our hotel owners, our shareholders, our customers, and our employees.

Source: Company data.

Exhibit 7   Comparative Data on Parisian Palaces

PROPERTY	CONSTRUCTION/STYLE	CAPACITY (ROOMS & SUITES)	AMENITIES	PRICE (U.S.$, PER SINGLE ROOM)	OWNER	LESSEE/OPERATOR
Bristol	Built in 1829 Louis XV–XVI style	180	1 restaurant: Le Bristol 1 interior garden 1 swimming pool 1 fitness center 1 beauty salon	480–600	Société Oetker[a] (1978)	Independent
Crillon	Built in the 18th century Louis XV–XVI style	152	2 restaurants: L'Ambassadeur and L'Obelix 1 fitness center Guerlain Beauty Institute	460–550	Groupe Hôtels Concorde[b] (1907)	Groupe Hôtels Concorde[b] (1907)
Four Seasons Hotel George V Paris	Built in 1928 Art Déco style	245	1 restaurant: Le Cinq 1 swimming pool 1 fitness center 1 beauty salon	670	Prince Al Waleed Bin Talal[c] (1996)	Four Seasons Hotels and Resorts (2000)
Meurice	Built in the 18th century Louis XV–XVI style	161	1 restaurant: Le Meurice 1 fitness center Caudalie Beauty Institute	470–550	The Sultan of Brunei (1997)	The Dorchester Group[d] (2001)
Plaza Athenée	Built in 1889 Belle Epoque style	144	2 restaurants: Le Relais Plaza	490–508	The Sultan of Brunei (1997)	The Dorchester Group[d] (2001)
Ritz	Built in 1898 Louis XV–XVI style	139	1 restaurant: L'espadon Escoffier-Ritz cooking school 1 fitness center 1 beauty salon 1 swimming pool	From 580	Mohammed Al Fayed (1979)	Independent

58

Sources: Brian D. Egger et al., "Four Seasons Hotels and Resorts," Crédit Suisse First Boston, April 5, 2002, p. 21. Also the following Web sites: <http://www.hotel-bristol.com>, <http://www.ritz.com>, <http://www.fourseasons.com/paris/vacations/index.html>, <http://www.plaza-athenee-paris.com>, <http://www.crillon.com>, accessed June 2002.

[a]The Oetker Group was a German agribusiness group that owned luxury hotels (including the Cap Eden Roc in Antibes, France; the Park Hotel in Vitznau, Switzerland; the Brenner's Park Hotel in Baden Baden, Germany; and the Château du Domaine Saint-Martin in Vence, France).

[b]Groupe Hôtels Concorde was created in 1973 to regroup the luxury hotels such as the Crillon, the Lutetia, and the Hotel Concorde Saint-Lazare (all in Paris) owned by La Société du Louvre.

[c]Al Waleed Bin Talal owned 21.9% of Four Seasons' stock. Investments by Prince Al Waleed in Four Seasons' properties included F. S. George V and Riyadh (100%); London (majority); Cairo, Amman, Alexandria, Sharm El Sheikh and Beirut (unspecified); and Aviara (minority).

[d]The Dorchester Group, a subsidiary of the Brunei Investment Agency, was established in 1996 as an independent U.K. registered company to manage luxury hotels, including The Dorchester in London, The Beverly Hills Hotel California, and the Hotel Meurice in Paris.

Exhibit 8   Predictable Patterns of Monochronic and Polychronic Cultures

Monochronic People (Americans)	Polychronic People (French)
Do one thing at a time.	Do many things at once.
Concentrate on the job.	Can be easily distracted and manage interruptions well.
Take time commitments (deadlines, schedules) seriously.	Consider an objective to be achieved, if possible.
Are low-context and need information.	Are high-context and already have information.
Are committed to the job.	Are committed to people and human relationships.
Adhere religiously to plans.	Change plans often and easily.
Are concerned about not disturbing others; follow rules of privacy and consideration.	Are more concerned with those who are closely related (family, friends, close business associates) than with privacy.
Show great respect for private property; seldom borrow or lend.	Borrow and lend things often and easily.
Emphasize promptness.	Base promptness on the relationship.
Are accustomed to short-term relationships.	Have strong tendency to build lifetime relationships.

Source: Adapted from Edward T. Hall, "Understanding Cultural Differences: Germans, French, and Americans" (Yarmouth, ME: Intercultural Press, 1990).

Exhibit 9   Employees-to-Room Ratios at Selected Four Seasons Properties

Property	Employees-to-Rooms Ratio
Four Seasons worldwide average	1.6
The Pierre New York	2.3
Four Seasons Hotel New York	1.6
Four Seasons Hotel George V Paris	2.5
Four Seasons Hotel Berlin	0.9
Four Seasons Hotel London	1.2
Four Seasons Hotel Canary Wharf, London	1.4
Four Seasons Hotel Milano	2.2

Source: Company data.

Endnotes

[1] *Interior Design*, March 2000, p. S24.

[2] For example, maternity leave for a salaried employee's first child was 6 weeks of prenatal leave and 10 weeks of paid leave after birth; for a third child it was 8 weeks off before and 18 weeks after birth.

[3] As of 2002, the Communist-controlled labor union (Confédération Générale du Travail or CGT) had nearly 2.4 million members (claimed); the independent labor union (Force Ouvrière) had 1 million members (est.); the independent white-collar union (Confédération Générale des Cadres) had 340,000 members (claimed); the Socialist-leaning labor union (Confédération Française Democratique du Travail or CFDT) had about 800,000 members (est.). Source: CIA Web site, <http://www.cia.gov/cia/ publications/factbook/geos/fr.html>, accessed June 10, 2002.

[4] Hofstede's work was based on a survey, conducted by questionnaire, of IBM employees in 50 different countries. See Geert Hofstede, *Culture's Consequences: International Differences in Work-related Values* (Thousand Oaks, CA: Sage, 1982).

[5] Hofstede's work has been criticized for the construction of the dimensions along which cultures differ. For example, D. Hickson comments (in "The ASQ Years Then and Now through the Eyes of a Euro-Brit," *Administrative Science Quarterly*, 41(2): 217–228) that Hofstede had "frail data, but robust concepts." However, there is general agreement with the principle that cultures do differ. Further, Hofstede's work and that of other scholars indicate that the differences between North American and French organizational culture are large.

[6] Philippe d'Iribarre, "The usefulness of an ethnographic approach to the international comparison of organization," *International Studies of Management and Organization*, 18(4): 32.

[7] Brian Van der Horst, "Edward T. Hall—A Great-Grandfather of NLP," <http://www.cs.ucr.edu/gnick/bvdh/ print_ edward_t_hall_great_.htm>, accessed April 20, 2002. The article reviews E. Hall, *The Silent Language* (New York: Doubleday, 1959).

[8] One alternative was to give the staff a significant enough severance package to encourage them to go. However, as Young explained, "the government deplores that approach."

[9] Usually used to describe a meal—say a first course of *fromage de tête* (pig's head set in jelly) or *bouillabaisse* (fish soup), followed by a main course of *blanquette de veau* (veal stew with white sauce) and rounded off with a *plateau de fromage* (cheese platter) or *tarte aux pommes* (apple tart).

BRIEF CASES

HARVARD
BUSINESS
SCHOOL
PUBLISHING

2073
JUNE 7, 2007

KAREN MARTINSEN FLEMING

Natureview Farm

It was a crisp Vermont morning in February 2000. Christine Walker, vice president of marketing for Natureview Farm, Inc., a small yogurt manufacturer, paused to collect her thoughts from a recently adjourned meeting with the other members of Natureview's senior management team. The team faced a challenging situation—that of finding a path to grow revenues by over 50% before the end of 2001. The central focus of the meeting was whether Natureview should expand into the supermarket channel in order to meet its revenue goal—a move which would represent a major departure from the company's established channel strategy and one which would impact every aspect of Natureview's business.

Despite the growth that Natureview Farm had been able to achieve since it began in 1989, the company had long struggled to maintain a consistent level of profitability. Jim Wagner, hired in 1996 as chief financial officer (CFO), had developed financial controls that brought steady profitability to the company, in line with dairy industry standards. No one at the firm had questioned Wagner's recommendation in 1997 that Natureview arrange for an equity infusion from a venture capital (VC) firm to fund strategic investments. However, the VC firm now needed to cash out of its investment in Natureview. Natureview management had to find another investor or position itself for acquisition, and increasing revenues was critical in order to attain the highest possible valuation[1] for the company. Wagner had advised the management that it would be critical to grow Natureview's revenues to $20 million before the end of 2001—a large jump from the $13 million the company reported in 1999. (See **Exhibit 1** for 1999 income statement.) While Wagner realized the bind Natureview was in, alternative financing would be extremely difficult until the VCs cashed out.

The previous day, Natureview's Chief Executive Officer (CEO) Barry Landers had admonished his management team that he needed a plan:

> We have to come up with a plan that takes us to $20 million in revenues by the end of 2001. This immediate pressure to grow the top line is going to help us get to the size that we have long aspired to be. As you think through our options, though, you can't lose sight of what has

---

[1] Organic foods companies similar to Natureview were frequently valued on a multiple of revenues rather than profit or cash flow because these VC firms were investing in order to generate significant revenue growth. Typical sales multiples ranged from 1.5 times to 2.1 times revenue, so maximizing overall revenue was critical to achieving a higher valuation by potential investors.

Karen Martinsen Fleming prepared this case solely as a basis for class discussion and not as an endorsement, a source of primary data, or an illustration of effective or ineffective management. An MBA from Harvard Business School, she has held marketing management positions at major consumer products companies. She currently teaches marketing courses and runs a consulting business in Vermont.

This case, though based on real events, is fictionalized, and any resemblance to actual persons or entities is coincidental. There are occasional references to actual companies in the narration.

made this company great. I'm proud of the strong brand we've built and what it represents in our marketplace, and I'm even more proud of the unconventional route we've taken to get here. We owe it to our customers, our suppliers, and our distribution partners to make the right strategic choices regarding the revenue growth objective before us.

Those words weighed heavily on the Natureview management team. The first meeting to address the CEO's challenge had not gone well. After much analysis and discussion, the team members were sharply divided.

Natureview Farm's Early Years and the Current Situation

Founded in 1989, Natureview Farm manufactured and marketed refrigerated cup yogurt under the Natureview Farm brand name. The yogurt was manufactured at the Natureview Farm production facility in Cabot, Vermont. The key to the Natureview yogurt flavor and texture was the family yogurt recipe developed by the company's founder. The recipe used natural ingredients and a special process that gave the yogurt its unique smooth, creamy texture without the artificial thickeners used by the major U.S. yogurt brands—Dannon, Yoplait, and Breyers. The company used milk from cows untreated with rGBH, an artificial growth hormone that increased milk production. Because of the special process and ingredients, Natureview Farm's yogurt's average shelf life (the length of time the yogurt stayed fresh) was 50 days. Most of the large competitors' products had a 30-day shelf life, requiring them to build multiple production plants to reduce shipping time to their distributors.

In 10 years, Natureview Farm's revenues had grown from less than $100,000 to $13 million. The company first entered the market with 8-ounce (oz.) and 32-oz. cup sizes of yogurt in two flavors—plain and vanilla. Based on its early success, the company added flavors to both sizes. The 8-oz. flavors were developed by putting fruit puree into the bottom of the cup and adding plain yogurt on top. Producing this "fruit on the bottom" yogurt product required new equipment, but it allowed the brand to expand its product offerings to help increase revenues. Because of the emphasis on natural ingredients and its strong reputation for high quality and great taste, the Natureview brand grew quickly to national distribution and shared leadership in the natural foods channel. This was aided by creative, low-cost "guerilla marketing" tactics that worked well in this channel.

By 2000, Natureview Farm produced twelve refrigerated yogurt flavors in 8-oz. cups (86% revenues) and four flavors in 32-oz. cups (14% revenues). The company had also started exploring multipack yogurt products (children's 4-oz. cups and yogurt packaged in tubes). Natureview shipped its yogurt to retailers in cases, with a typical case containing 12 cups for the 8-oz. and 6 cups for the 32-oz. product lines, respectively. (If the company were to expand into multipack products, their cases would contain four packages.) As a major brand in the natural foods channel, Natureview Farm had developed strong relationships with leading natural foods retailers, including the chains Whole Foods ($1.57 billion revenues in 1999) and Wild Oats ($721 million revenues). The organic foods market, worth $6.5 billion in 1999, was predicted to grow to $13.3 billion in 2003.[2]

The Refrigerated Yogurt Category and the Yogurt Consumer

Yogurt is a dairy product, the result of milk fermented in a carefully controlled environment. Special bacteria added to the milk change its texture and give yogurt its unique health properties—it

---

[2] "A Step Closer To Defining 'Organic,'" *Natural Foods Merchandiser* 12: 43 (December 1999).

is a good source of calcium and improves digestion. Plain yogurt is typically made from whole, low-fat, or nonfat milk without additional flavoring ingredients. Flavored yogurt has sugar and either artificial flavorings or natural fruit (or both) added.

In 1999, total U.S. retail sales of refrigerated yogurt reached $1.8 billion and sales volume was just over 2.3 billion units. The market was fairly concentrated with the top four competitors—Dannon, Yoplait, Breyers, and Columbo—having the dominant share and the top two competitors controlling over 50% of the market. In 1999, when sales through the dominant two distribution channels—supermarkets and natural foods stores—were combined, supermarkets sold 97% of all yogurt consumed, and natural food stores sold the balance. Yogurt revenues were also generated through other channels, including warehouse clubs, convenience stores, drug stores, and mass merchandisers. However, Natureview did not consider entry into these channels because, relative to the supermarket channel, these channels offered limited revenue generation potential; the company's product was not a strong fit for the narrow product offering afforded to consumers through these channels; and volume requirements were prohibitive in certain channels. Warehouse clubs, for example, required multiple unit packages, 24 cups of 8-oz. cups per carton, but Natureview did not view its brand as developed enough to generate the consumer demand necessary to meet this volume requirement. In the previous five years, yogurt sales through supermarkets had grown an average of 3% per year, while sales through natural food stores had grown 20% per year. Because consumers were increasingly interested in natural and organic foods, well-managed natural foods retailers were thriving. Yogurt was an important product in the overall dairy portfolio of natural foods retailers, since stores earned a higher margin on yogurt than on any other dairy product.

Shoppers at natural foods stores tended to be more educated, earn higher incomes, and be older than the typical supermarket shopper. Forty-six percent of organic food consumers bought organic products at a supermarket, 25% at a small health foods store, and 29% at a natural foods supermarket. Generally, shoppers who purchased organic products, regardless of channel, tended to have higher incomes, have more education, and live in the Northeast and West. Organic dairy products were bought by 74% of heavy organic food buyers and 29% of light organic food buyers. Sixty-seven percent of U.S. households indicated that price was a barrier to their purchase of organic products, and 58% expressed that they would buy more organic product if it were less expensive. Forty-four percent of consumers identified the need for a wider selection of organic product in supermarkets.[3]

Yogurt was consumed by approximately 40% of the U.S. population, with women comprising the majority (over 70%) of yogurt purchases. Factors considered when deciding which yogurt to purchase included package type/size, taste, flavor, price, freshness, ingredients, and whether the product was organic, typically in that order of preference. For natural foods shoppers, the product's ingredients and whether or not the product was organic were more important purchase criteria. Among natural foods shoppers, a product's health-promoting qualities were usually more important than price in the purchase decision.

Regarding consumer product preferences, 6- and 8-oz. yogurt cups were the most popular product sizes, representing 74% of total category supermarket sales in U.S. dollars. This segment was growing 3% per year, but also faced stiff competition. Women primarily bought 8-oz. yogurt cups as a healthy snack or lunch substitute and valued a variety of flavors since most consumers did not "add" anything to this size. By comparison, the next largest segment—multipacks—represented 9% of category sales and was growing by more than 12.5% per year. Children (and their mothers,

---

[3] "A Step Closer To Defining 'Organic,'" *Natural Foods Merchandiser* 12: 43 (December 1999); "Organic Products Are On One Third of Shopping Lists Enhanced Title," Research Alert 18(7):5 (April 07, 2000); eBrain Market Research, http://www.ebrain.org/ (2002 survey).

seeking healthier snack alternatives) were the target of the fastest growing multipacks. These included six-packs of 4-oz. cup servings and the "fun and less messy" tube yogurt, which was squeezed from a flexible plastic tube and could be eaten without a spoon; eight 2-oz. tubes were included in the typical multipack. The last segment, the 32-oz. size, represented 8% of sales and was growing at a modest 2%. Buyers of the 32-oz. size were "heavy" yogurt consumers, who either ate the yogurt plain, added other ingredients (granola, fruit, etc.), or used yogurt in recipes (smoothies, cooking). For the 32-oz. size, the most popular flavors were plain and vanilla, and the most important purchase criteria were brand, expiration date, and price. (See **Exhibit 2** for yogurt market share by segment and region in the supermarket channel.)

Stores typically merchandised yogurt product in their own section within the refrigerated dairy case. The size of the yogurt section varied from store to store, although on average, the yogurt section in a natural foods store was smaller (4' wide by 6' high) than that in a supermarket (8' wide by 6' high). In both channels, the small cups (6-oz. and 8-oz.) were displayed on the upper two shelves, most commonly at eye level—where consumers more often purchased items, research showed. Stores usually put multipacks on the next-lowest shelves and 32-oz. containers in the bottom "well" (the least visible spot).

The Sales and Distribution Process:
Supermarket Channel vs. Natural Foods Stores

Supermarket Channel

Large consumer products manufacturers, such as Procter & Gamble and Coca Cola, had dedicated sales forces that called directly on category buyers who ultimately controlled dairy product placement in their stores. By contrast, smaller manufacturers like Natureview Farms used sales brokers to sell their yogurt to both natural foods and supermarket chains. These influential brokers, representing several brands of consumer products, used their relationships to arrange discussions between retail chains, wholesalers, and manufacturers, in addition to performing numerous other services for manufacturers. For these services, brokers charged manufacturers such as Natureview a fee or commission that varied from product to product. For yogurt, the broker's fee was 4% of manufacturer's sales.[4]

If Natureview Farm chose to expand into the supermarket channel, it would depend heavily on its broker's knowledge of promotional and merchandising requirements. For each item or SKU (stock-keeping unit) they carried, supermarket chains aimed to maximize sales volume and inventory turns.

Supermarkets carefully monitored sales trends, especially of new items, by region, area, and store, using sophisticated scanner technology. Their relatively streamlined distribution systems also allowed supermarkets to maintain lower prices. Suppliers to supermarkets typically sent products to a large distribution center, which in turn shipped directly to the supermarket chain's warehouse. This facilitated efficient distribution to the individual stores. At each step, the distributor and the retailer charged a markup on products that flowed through their warehouses or stores. The typical distributor margin in this channel was 15%, and the typical retailer margin was 27%. These margins were consistent across yogurt product type. A supermarket would charge $0.74 for the same cup of yogurt priced at $0.88 in a natural foods store. (See **Exhibit 3** for manufacturing costs and retail prices by channel.)

---

[4] Broker's fees were typically accounted for in SG&A (Sales, General & Administrative) expense.

In order to sell its yogurt into supermarkets, Natureview would be required to pay a one-time "slotting fee" for each SKU only in the first year it was introduced and then to participate in regular trade promotions—both uncommon practices in the natural foods channel. The supermarket retailer charged this slotting fee in order to set up a slot throughout its distribution system for the new SKU and then monitor its sales trends. If the SKU did not prove profitable for the supermarket within the year, the supermarket would discontinue the product and would require a new slotting fee payment in the event the manufacturer sought reauthorization of the SKU. For refrigerated yogurt, the slotting fee averaged $10,000 per SKU per retail chain. For instance, Natureview would need to pay each supermarket chain $80,000 to introduce eight different flavors in the 8-oz. size.

Once an item became part of a supermarket chain's regular inventory, the chain expected or required the manufacturer to participate in regular trade promotions, usually at least every three months. This meant advertising the product in the weekly sales circular that the supermarket distributed to local households. The cost of trade promotion ads varied widely by region and by size of the advertisement. In the Northeast, Midwest, and Southeast of the U.S., advertisements cost $7,500 for the size typically used by Natureview Farm's competitors. In the West, the same advertisements cost $15,000 per ad per retailer. (Nationally, they cost $8,000 on average.) While these were not significant expenses for larger competitors such as Dannon and Yoplait, both of which spent over $60 million per year in marketing their yogurt products, this was an expensive proposition for smaller manufacturers to match.

Natural Foods Channel

Natural foods chains typically charged higher retail prices for the same products than supermarkets did, due to lower price sensitivity among natural foods customers as well as differences in the distribution system. Distribution in the natural foods channel involved four, instead of three, parties. A manufacturer like Natureview first shipped products to a natural foods wholesaler. The wholesaler shipped the yogurt to a natural foods distributor, who in turn delivered the products to a retailer like Whole Foods. (See **Exhibit 4** for a diagram illustrating the length of each channel to market.) In contrast to supermarket distributors, intermediaries in the natural foods channel would "break cases" (i.e., allow natural foods retailers, who tended to be small stores at the time, organized in few chains) to order fewer items than a full case. Furthermore, natural foods distributors would deliver product to individual stores, and in some instances even stock the shelves and track paperwork. The typical natural foods wholesaler margin was 7%, the distributor margin was 9%, and the retailer margin was 35%. These margins tended to be consistent across yogurt product type. Thus, by the time an 8-oz. cup of yogurt had reached the store shelf in the natural foods channel, it had passed through two distribution points plus the retailer, and the retail price of the 8-oz. cup was $0.88.

In contrast to supermarket chains, natural foods retailers did not charge manufacturers monetary slotting fees, but did require a one-time allotment of one free case of product for every new SKU authorized for distribution in its first year. Aside from the large chains—Whole Foods and Wild Oats—most natural foods stores lacked automated scanner checkout systems to track sales from promotions, and price discounts were usually not necessary to achieve sales targets. The competitors that Natureview faced in the natural foods channel versus the supermarket channel reflected the different business models, consumer audiences, and distribution systems inherent in both channels. Horizon Organic, flush with cash from a recent initial public offering (IPO), was Natureview's greatest competitor to obtaining supermarket distribution. It produced a full range of organic dairy products and was a national brand in natural foods stores. Brown Cow was a smaller company with a strong regional presence on the West Coast. Brown Cow's yogurt was "all natural," but not organic; Horizon's was organic, but it had a shorter shelf life than Natureview's product. (See **Exhibit 5** for market share by brand.)

The Senior Management Team's Three Options

Back in her office, Christine Walker was considering the three options that the senior management team had proposed to grow Natureview's revenues to $20 million by the end of 2001. Two of the options required Natureview to enter the supermarket channel. While supermarket distribution offered Natureview a potential solution to its revenue requirement, it also presented potential problems that required careful evaluation.[5] She wondered what would it really take to thrive in the supermarket channel. The ripple effect of this decision could shake Natureview to its core, changing all aspects of Walker's job, from how she allocated marketing budgets to how she thought about brand strategy.

What concerned Walker even more was the CEO's admonition that kept ringing in her head. "We owe it to our customers, our suppliers, and our distribution partners to make the right strategic choices regarding this revenue growth objective." Natureview accounted for 24% of yogurt sales through the natural foods channel. These retailers had made Natureview what it was today. How would these long-term partners react to seeing Natureview's yogurt at the supermarket down the street at prices at least 15% lower? Would price concessions follow? Worse yet, would the stores in Natureview's traditional channel drop the brand and replace it with competitors' lines? When Natureview's current broker heard about the plan, he would likely let everyone at the company know his displeasure. Clearly Walker would have to minimize the damage to the channel support Natureview had established.

Walker picked up her notebook, which summarized the three options. Fortunately, none of them required building a new facility in the short term, which would have cost $30 million, and capital expenditures for manufacturing were approximately equal across the three options.

Option 1

The first option, to expand six SKUs of the 8-oz. product line into one or two selected supermarket channel regions, was most strongly advocated by Walter Bellini, vice president of sales. (Pursuing six SKUs struck the right balance between having enough cups on the shelf to provide a good shelf presence, while not incurring too large a slotting expense. The six SKUs chosen were the best-selling SKUs of the 8-oz. line.) His argument was based on four key points:

1. Eight-ounce cups represented the largest dollar and unit share of the refrigerated yogurt market, providing significant revenue potential.

2. Other natural foods brands had successfully expanded their distribution into the supermarket channel. Two such brands—Silk Soymilk and Amy's Organic Foods—had increased revenues by over 200% within two years of entering supermarkets. Natureview, the leading natural foods brand of refrigerated yogurt, was uniquely positioned to capitalize on the growing trend in natural and organic foods in supermarkets.

3. Bellini had heard rumors that one of Natureview's major natural foods competitors would soon try to expand into the supermarket channel. Supermarket retailers would likely

---

[5] Natureview used a discount rate of 8% to evaluate projects.

authorize only one organic yogurt brand. The first brand to enter the channel could therefore have a significant first-mover advantage.

One of Natureview's brokers had told Bellini that supermarket chains—afraid of losing market share to other channels—believed that offering more organic products in their stores would attract higher-income, less price-sensitive customers. Bellini mentioned that some industry experts were predicting unit volume growth of organic yogurt at supermarkets of 20% per year from 2001 to 2006. These predictions were relative to unit growth projections of 2% to 4% for the yogurt category overall in the supermarket channel.

The team acknowledged that this option had great upside potential but also higher risks and costs. The 8-oz. size received the highest level of competitive trade promotion and marketing spending. Natureview Farm's sales broker had indicated that supporting this cup size would require quarterly trade promotions and a meaningful marketing budget. Natureview's advertising agency estimated that a comprehensive advertising plan (comprising television, radio, outdoor, and print advertising) would cost Natureview $1.2 million per region per year. These launch expenditures were in addition to the trade promotion expenditures the company would need to make. Natureview's sales, general, and administrative expenses (SG&A) would increase by $320,000 annually; $200,000 would be incremental SG&A for additions to sales staff required to manage the supermarket brokers in the two regions, and $120,000 would go towards additional marketing staff.

With this level of advertising support, Natureview felt it could achieve a 1.5% share of supermarket yogurt sales after one year, producing an incremental annual sales volume of just over 35 million units. (See **Exhibit 6** for incremental unit sales projections by strategic option.) This projection also assumed Natureview's brokers could take advantage of their relationships with the top 11 supermarket retail chains in the Northeast and the top 9 chains in the West. Research showed that supermarket consumers in the northeastern and western regions were more likely to purchase organic and natural foods than consumers in other regions.

Walker found Bellini's arguments compelling. It was hard to counter his belief that Natureview had to enter the supermarket channel to successfully address the revenue gap. For Bellini, the "go or no-go" decision was clearly a question of "when" and "how," not "if." Walker glanced down at her notebook again.

Option 2

The second option—to expand four SKUs of the 32-oz. size nationally—was advocated by Jack Gottlieb, vice president of operations. His argument was based on four key points:

1. Although 32-oz. cups comprised a smaller unit and dollar share of the yogurt market, they currently generated an above-average gross profit margin for Natureview (43.6% vs. 36.0% for the 8-oz. line).

2. There were fewer competitive offerings in this size, and Natureview Farm had a strong competitive advantage because of the product's longer shelf life. Natureview's brand had achieved a 45% share of this size segment in the natural foods channel. The management team felt that it was realistic to assume that the company could sell approximately 5.5 million incremental units in the first year. To generate this projection, Natureview's broker advised that the company would need to expand into 64 supermarket retail chains across the United States.

3. Although slotting expenses would be higher because national distribution would require slotting fees across a larger number of retailers, promotional expenses would be lower—the 32-oz. size was promoted only twice a year.   For a 32-oz. expansion, marketing expenses would be significantly lower as well—only 10% of what was projected for the 8-oz. size in each region, representing $120,000 per region per year.

Despite the many advantages of this option, the management team doubted that new users would readily "enter the brand" via a multi-use size. Bellini was also concerned about his sales team's ability to achieve full national distribution in just 12 months. Furthermore, as with the first option, Natureview would need to hire sales personnel who had experience selling to the more sophisticated supermarket channel and would need to establish relationships with supermarket brokers. Additions to sales headcount for the 32-oz. expansion option would increase SG&A by $160,000.

Despite these concerns, Walker thought this was an interesting option to consider. Dannon was rumored to be launching a line called Bright Vista, an organic yogurt that would compete directly with Natureview. Supermarkets themselves were also considering launching their own private-label versions of organic yogurt. Would launching a 32-oz. offering be less noticed by the competition? Could it acquaint supermarket customers with the brand before Natureview pursued the 8-oz. size in the supermarket channel? Since the 8-oz. size was the "bread and butter" product for Natureview's competitors, they might view an expansion into the 8-oz. market as a greater threat by Natureview.

Option 3

The third option—to introduce two SKUs of a children's multi-pack into the natural foods channel— was advocated by Walker's colleague Kelly Riley, the assistant marketing director. Riley based her argument on five key points:

1. The company already had strong relationships with the leading natural foods channel retailers, and expansion into the supermarket channel could potentially affect these relationships. Yogurt was an important product to natural foods retailers from both a revenue and a profit standpoint.

2. Riley also was not convinced that Natureview had the necessary resources or skill-set to sell effectively to and through supermarkets. Her recent conversations with Natureview's brokers, who were skeptical of the move, had only added to her concerns, and she feared that her colleagues were not adequately taking into account the impact that a "go" decision would have on the current marketing, sales, brand, and channel-partner arrangements.

3. Natureview Farm's all-natural ingredients would provide the perfect positioning from which to launch its own children's multi-pack product offering into their core sales channel. The sales team was confident that they could achieve distribution for the two SKUs.

4. The financial potential was very attractive. The projected total yearly revenue for the two multipack SKUs would be approximately 10% of the natural foods channel category dollar sales, and Riley estimated potential incremental unit volume at 1.8 million. Gross profitability of the line would be 37.6%. Furthermore, sales and marketing expenses in this channel were lower; the cost of the complimentary cases was estimated at 2.5% of the product line's manufacturer sales, and the marketing expenses were estimated at $250,000. Riley believed that introducing this product line into the natural foods channel would yield the strongest profit contribution of all the strategies under consideration.

5. The natural foods channel was growing almost seven times faster than the supermarket channel, and Natureview was developing several new products that could further boost sales performance in this highly successful channel. The five-year projected unit growth CAGR of yogurt in the natural foods channel was projected to be 15%, according to industry market research.

For this option, R&D and Operations would need to develop the multipack product. Natureview would incur no additional SG&A costs to introduce the multipack product—this was within the capabilities of the current functional resources.

While the management team sympathized with Riley's concerns, the team argued that potential channel conflict should not be the deciding factor—Natureview could find ways to manage it. But Riley held firm to her belief that supermarkets' emphasis on sales promotion and price was inconsistent with the premium brand positioning that Walker and Riley had worked hard to establish. Walker also recalled Riley describing her fear that Natureview's marketing department was unprepared to handle the demands on resources and staffing that entering the supermarket channel would impose.

Walker thought back to the exploratory conversation she and Riley had not long ago with a dairy buyer at a large Boston-based supermarket chain. He had advised them, "You're going to have to show us a real marketing plan if you want us to distribute your brand. Trade promotion spending and clever public relations stunts alone aren't going to cut it." She also remembered the previous day's conversation with Natureview's fulfillment manager, who had raised concerns about Natureview's ability to handle distribution to supermarket distributors. Such distributors were more demanding from a logistical and technological standpoint compared with distribution partners Natureview was familiar with from the natural foods channel. Instead of incurring the inevitable cost, change, and trauma from entering the supermarket channel, Kelly Riley wanted Natureview to focus on the "shooting star" and create a strategy to gain shelf space at natural foods retailers. Riley could be right, Walker thought, but she also suspected that the natural foods channel would soon be making demands much like those that Riley feared from supermarkets. Walker knew from experience that retailers were likely to demand more and more as they grew.

Just then, the phone rang. It was Natureview's CEO. "Christine, I'm really counting on you to help us figure out what to do here. I trust your instincts about the marketplace—our customers, competitors, and channels. You have the best direct read on all of this, and I need a coherent point of view and an action plan. I know these are not easy decisions, but I have confidence that you'll lead us down the right path."

Exhibit 1 Natureview Farm Income Statement, 1999

Revenues[a]	$13,000,000	100% Revenues
Cost of Goods Sold[b]	$ 8,190,000	63%
Gross Profit	$ 4,810,000	37%
Expenses		
- Administration/Freight	$ 2,210,000	17%
- Sales	$ 1,560,000	12%
- Marketing	$ 390,000	3%
- Research & Development	$ 390,000	3%
Net Income	$ 260,000	2%

[a]Natureview's 1999 revenues were 100% generated from sales of refrigerated yogurt to natural foods stores.

[b]The COGS reflects a product mix of 86% 8-oz. yogurt cups and 14% 32-oz. yogurt cups.

Exhibit 2 Yogurt Market Share by Packaging Segment, 1999
(Supermarket channel, in % U.S. dollars)

	Dollar Share	Dollar Sales Change vs. Prior Year
8-oz. cups and smaller	74%	+3%
Children's multipacks	9%	+12.5%
32-oz. cups	8%	+2%
Other	9%	NC
	100%	

Yogurt Market Share by Region, 1999
(Supermarket channel, in % U.S. dollars)

	Dollar Share	No. of Retailers in the Region
Northeast	26%	25
Midwest	22%	30
Southeast	25%	33
West	27%	17
	100%	

Note: Market share is given as percentage U.S. dollars for national U.S. market.

Exhibit 3   Yogurt Production Costs and Retail Prices by Channel

Natural Foods Channel	Average Retail Price
8-ounce (oz.) cup	$ 0.88
32-oz. cup	$ 3.19
4- oz. cup multipack	$ 3.35

Supermarket Channel	Average Retail Price
8-oz. cup	$ 0.74
32-oz. cup	$ 2.70
4-oz. cup multipack	$ 2.85

Note: Natureview's manufacturing costs for the three product lines—the 8-oz. cup, the 32-oz. cup, and the children's multipack—were $0.31, $0.99, and $1.15 respectively.

Exhibit 4   Length of Channels to Market

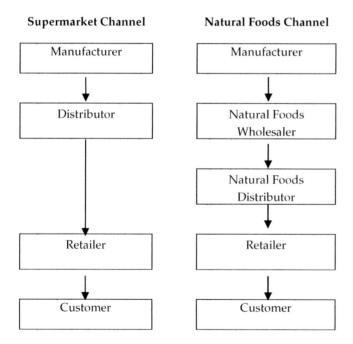

Exhibit 5 Yogurt Market Share by Brand, 1999
(Supermarket and Natural Foods channels, in % U.S. dollars)

Supermarket Channel

Dannon	33%
Yoplait	24%
Others	23%
Private Label	15%
Columbo	5%
	100%

Natural Foods Channel

Natureview Farm	24%
Brown Cow	15%
Horizon Organic	19%
White Wave	7%
Others	35%
	100%

Exhibit 6 Sales Projections for Natureview's Strategic Options

Option	Action	Anticipated Incremental Retail Unit Sales
1	Expand 6 SKUs of the 8-oz. size into eastern and western supermarket regions	35,000,000
2	Expand 4 SKUs of the 32-oz. size nationally into supermarket channel	5,500,000
3	Introduce 2 children's multipacks into natural foods channel	1,800,000

9B01M011

QUEST FOODS ASIA PACIFIC AND THE CRM INITIATIVE

"Declan, we have to talk," said Mathijs Boeren, marketing director Foods, Asia Pacific, Quest International, as he walked into the Singapore office of Declan MacFadden, regional vice-president, Foods, Asia Pacific, in the early morning of February 28, 2000. Quest, which among other activities created flavors and textures for food and beverage companies, had about six months earlier begun implementing a business process re-engineering (BPR) project. This initiative involved the analysis of every facet of Quest's businesses with the objective of finding new and better ways of operating.

MacFadden was responsible for the implementation of the Foods Division BPR throughout Asia Pacific. As part of this effort, he was also championing the development of an information technology-based customer relationship management model (CRM), an initiative he felt was critical for Quest to gain a sustainable competitive advantage with customers in the region. This initiative would offer much more to customers than the company's current Web site, where customers could simply obtain basic information on Quest's global operations and product offerings. Likely, it would contain interactive communications with some processes handled without human contact. MacFadden's ultimate goal was to bring Quest to the next phase of e-business — full interactivity.

Boeren took a seat and began talking:

> Declan, I've just come from a meeting with International Snackfoods.[1] The director of Procurement for Asia Pacific, Larry Wong, told me that one of our most formidable competitors had implemented CRM technology weeks earlier. Though Wong was somewhat reticent, he did hint to me that the new system addressed some of International Snackfoods' needs for increased transparency, responsiveness and information flow. As far as I can tell, this new system not only tracks orders, but is likely the first stage of a full Extranet. If so, our competitor will be able to give our key customers increased transparency, accelerate their product development, and link their research and development (R&D) facilities before we can.
>
> As you can well imagine, this makes me nervous. At this point, I don't know whether our competitor has implemented this system worldwide. But whether it has or not, I am still concerned about Quest's 'mission readiness' for a similar IT platform.

MacFadden sank back into his chair. He already felt pressure to move forward with CRM, hearing through the grapevine that some senior managers felt that the project was moving too slowly. But this pressure was not universal. In a recent regional directors' meeting, others had questioned whether CRM was even a worthwhile priority given the finite time and money resources available, especially if its development and implementation ran concurrent to the implementation of Quest's BPR.

"Still, Mathijs," MacFadden said, "the issue remains — what are our priorities?" MacFadden, Boeren and the executive team in charge of the implementation of Quest's BPR had considered the implications to that question for months. Although the elements of an initial CRM had been created, it was still in its early stages. And, although some of Quest's customers had expressed interest in using a CRM system, it remained unclear whether a fully deployed CRM would generate any new sales.

After Boeren had left his office, MacFadden swiveled his chair, and took in the view of Singapore's financial district, contemplating the situation. Should he wait until the key components of the BPR process had been smoothly implemented, or should he respond to a potential need in the market and rush through the process of setting up a CRM? If the latter, should he focus the CRM initiative on just one customer in one region, one customer globally, or should he involve all customers that might be interested? Beyond this decision was the concern over the degree of

---

[1]International Snackfoods is a disguised name for a large, U.S.-based manufacturer of convenience food products.

sophistication offered by the system? The greater the sophistication, the longer the development time. The simpler the system, the less interest customers might have. Although MacFadden believed wholeheartedly that a CRM system could potentially hold the key to Quest's long-term competitive advantage, he was clearly troubled as to how he should proceed.

THE FOOD FLAVORING INDUSTRY

Consumers around the world had an almost insatiable appetite for new flavors incorporated into either new or existing products. Distinctive flavors had always given food and beverage manufacturers their competitive edge, and consumer demands for more convenient, healthful foods put enormous pressure on the flavorings industry for new and innovative products. Most flavor houses combined a wide range of artificial and natural products with a family of emulsifiers and stabilizers that provided "texture" for the food. Texture was important in creating "mouth feel" — for example, whether the final food product was creamy, sticky or smooth.

The flavorings industry consisted of two different market segments: the generic market (off-the-shelf flavors), and the custom flavoring market, which Quest focused on. Although occasionally Quest would approach its clients with a need that was identified through their marketing or R&D channels, responding to a customer's request for a particular product ingredient or flavoring generated the vast majority of its business.

In order to delineate the desired performance parameters of their new or improved product, food manufacturers issued a "brief" to Quest and other ingredients suppliers. Responding to the brief generally took between three to six months, and was a non-recoverable expense. At the deadline date, each company responding to the brief presented the specific performance details of its formulation to the client. Once accepted by a customer, the formulation that was developed could not be used for any other customer (though it remained the developer's intellectual property). Clients demanded strict confidentiality.

DELIVERING INCREASED VALUE-ADDED SERVICES

Boeren explained Quest's business model:

> We don't sell finished products. Quest sells food ingredients and flavors that are incorporated with other food components to become an end product. In this business you must have a core competency in the application of your products in a final food product. We cannot just give our customers large bags of white powder, and say

'here it is.' It's very important that we understand how our customers are using the ingredient. Moreover, achieving the desired performance or taste in a lab is usually very different from replicating it in a mass manufacturing environment. Flavor houses need real expertise in the scalability of their developments.

Over the past few years, global food and beverage manufacturers had leveraged their considerable purchasing clout, and had begun to ask for — and receive — more value-added services from their suppliers. According to MacFadden:

Increasingly our customers want us to move further down the value chain and have Quest deliver to them something new. We are now becoming increasingly responsible for determining trends in consumer preferences, finding new flavors and flavor substances, discovering new ingredients that maintain the integrity of the flavor.

Within the last three or four years, customers have been saying to Quest: 'Show me that you've got a winning new flavor — show me quantitative evidence for the preference for the flavor by consumers.' They've even begun to prescribe what type of statistical market analysis they want done.

Recognizing that Quest would lose credibility if it developed flavors that scored very low on consumer taste tests or if the products were taken off the market soon after introduction, Quest was strongly committed to conducting market research for its clients. Moreover, given that consumer tastes and demands always evolved, Quest was constantly seeking new ways to stay in tune with the market and enhance or refine existing products, or meet new consumer needs. Quest's extensive marketing research department provided key market information, including data on consumption patterns, trends, industry structure, and more importantly on consumer tastes and preferences, for various regions throughout the world. This was happening at a time when Quest's customers were becoming increasingly price-sensitive (most markedly in MacFadden's region since the onset of the Asian financial crisis). Thus, Quest (and its competitors) faced considerable pressure to develop ingredients and applications that were not only low cost but that delivered high efficacy.

With a view to eliminating redundancies and creating increased economies of scale, many of Quest's largest customers were globally organizing procurement, manufacturing, operational and administrative processes, as well as developing global brands. Despite these trends, strong national and regional differences continued in the area of food flavorings and textures. Cheese flavor, for example, could have many different nuances — a spicy flavor in India and Indonesia or fish flavor in Japan. Even though large companies like International Snackfoods had invested heavily in global brands and global purchasing systems, when it came to matters of flavors and food textures, they faced the reality that subtle — and in some cases, distinct — demand differences existed from country to country.

THE COMPETITIVE LANDSCAPE

A dozen or so globally aligned companies dominated the food ingredients and flavors industry (comprised of hundreds of smaller firms). Companies that manufactured flavors and texturising products were generally thought of as representing the highest value-added segment of the overall food ingredients industry.

Because of the role of chemical sciences and biotechnology in the flavorings industry, many industry players had strong ties to large, well-funded agricultural, chemical, and pharmaceutical companies. Quest's major competitors included Givaudan Roure (a division of the large Swiss-based pharmaceutical company Hoffman La Roche), Firmenich (also Swiss-based), New York-based International Flavors & Fragrances (IFF), and several major Japanese players including Takasako and Hasegawa. Increasingly, large chemicals and pharmaceutical companies were divesting non-core assets including their flavors and textures businesses. Some industry observers expected that these divestments would continue, followed over the next ten years by consolidation in the industry, resulting eventually in three or four huge global players.

The natural interdependence between the developers of flavors and textures and the food manufacturers themselves was expected to forge increasingly strong partnerships in the future. A noticeable trend was the blurring of boundaries between developer and manufacturer with arrangements including exclusive or preferential development and collaborative joint ventures. A prime example of this relationship was Frito-Lay's alliance with Procter and Gamble, which resulted in the development of a synthetic fat named Olestra for snack foods.

Another element altering the structure of the industry was a dramatic reduction in development times and a rapid stream of new products and ingredients, which made innovation more imperative than ever. MacFadden explained Quest's commitment with regard to innovation:

> The relationship we have developed and nurtured over the years with our key customers gets us into their labs to work on solutions together. We need to constantly design creative solutions to the problems they bring to us. The key to success is coming up with revolutionary ideas.

Though innovations vary around the world, many are really product line extensions — mostly ethnic line extensions in the Western consumer markets. But, in countries like Japan, there is also phenomenal innovation, including new flavors, new foods, and nutritional benefits.

In the past, researchers and marketers were essentially taking 'bad' elements out of food, like fats and sugar. Now they are working on adding back 'good' things — nutrients, fiber, and so on —to produce what are called 'functional foods.' Producers are also pushing convenience-food solutions — products that are prepared faster, with higher nutritional value, and that are more shelf-stable. These concepts are starting to spread worldwide.

QUEST INTERNATIONAL

Quest was based in Naarden, Holland and was a major division of UK-based ICI. By 1999, ICI employed almost 60,000 people worldwide, and sold over £5.6 billion of products, resulting in a net profit (before goodwill, amortization and exceptional items) of £267 million. Quest's 4,000 employees developed and manufactured an extensive product line that included not only flavors and textures, but also fragrances for perfume manufacturers of cosmetics, toiletries, dental products and household goods. In 1999, due to rising sales and further operational efficiencies, Quest realized a profit of £92 million on sales of £676 million, more than 18 per cent more than the previous year.[2]

Flavorings and textures were part of the Food Division, which was organized around (1) products, (2) end users, and (3) geography. Quest's Food Division developed products for several categories, including the dairy and beverage industries, bakery and confectionery products, meals, soups, sauces and dressings, snack foods, meats, human nutrition, and cell nutrition (see Exhibit 1). In total, the Food Division had six different product groups, four end users (bakery, savory, beverage, dairy), and four geographic regions. Some observers wondered whether the Division's organizational structure was overly complex in an industry that was becoming increasingly global and where the ability to generate synergies was growing rapidly.

In 1999, Quest's Food Division grew at five per cent, ahead of the market, with flavors doing particularly well. Many observers attributed the success of Quest's Food Division to its ability to leverage its global network, marketing acumen, and its use of world-class R&D and application skills. Top managers were proud of the Division's culture which encouraged regional managers, scientists and account managers to work together to seek creative answers to the challenges they faced.

---

[2]In February 2000, £1.0 = US$1.55.

Senior employees were generally empowered to seek their own solutions, and many had developed close relationships with customers by creating special formulations that were especially effective.

QUEST'S BPR PROCESS

BPR represented an attempt to better serve customers by streamlining international operations. Within the Food Division, BPR represented a fundamental rethinking and radical redesign of business processes to achieve dramatic improvements in critical measures of performance, including cost, quality, service and speed. The implementation of Quest's BPR had begun about six months earlier, after having obtained Board level support. Such high level support was critical, given the scope and strategic shift the initiative involved.

A new business model was at the heart of the BPR process, and the challenge was to find one that would truly differentiate Quest from its competitors. Paul Drechsler, chairman and CEO, Quest International, commented on the importance and direction of BPR:

Having exited Y2K and looked at our priorities over the next two years, BPR is one of eight priorities we have set. Interestingly, BPR is a key enabler of the other seven initiatives, so it is important to us. At this stage, the over-riding priority is to strengthen our customer-driven focus. I am very flexible about the design and possibilities for BPR. I don't have a predisposed view of what it should look like. However, I can say that whatever we do has to be earnings enhancing. I need to deliver BPR without a one-year financial dip.

MacFadden was excited by the emphasis on customer intimacy and Quest's openness to new business models. He saw the BPR process as "not just a case of improving what we currently have." He continued,

We have set an ambitious goal to double revenue within about five years and to strengthen our relationship with our valued customers around the globe. BPR can play a pivotal role in this process by helping us revolutionize our operations.

Our first step is to align all our processes so that everybody works the same way, using the same processes. This means standardizing operations management, administrative and customer services functions, for example — every facet of the company — so that it is the same no matter which Quest operation you're working at. We are forecasting this will be a US$70 million to US$80 million project, which will take between two to three years to complete.

MacFadden's work on BPR put him in regular contact with various key managers from the Asia Division head office in Singapore, as well as Quest's four regional directors in Asia, one each for Australia and New Zealand, Japan and Korea, China, and all other Southeast Asian nations (based in Jakarta). Dreschler commented on the selection of MacFadden for this role:

Each food executive takes charge of a key project or process around the business. MacFadden was given BPR because he really wanted to do it. He was hungry for it. In my view, we need a bias for action more than intellectual conversion.

KNOWLEDGE MANAGEMENT AT QUEST

A critical goal of BPR was a new ability to share data on best practices, competitors, and customers on a global basis. Quest relied on two methods of storing knowledge — in "employees' brains," and through the process of codifying data (either electronically, or through a written record). MacFadden explained:

The majority of our processes are documented, somewhere or other, throughout the world. Our major challenge is to get this information into the hands of the people who need it. However, the reality is that getting it organized, codified and entered into compatible databases is a hell of a job.

Critical information in the Food Division was shared across geographies through word of mouth, documented processes, and cross-functional teams. On occasion, a specialist in a particular application — cheese flavoring on crackers, for instance — would visit the development team (located anywhere in the world) to apply his or her expertise personally to the brief. However, this had obvious time, space, and money resource restraints. As a result, the quality of information exchange varied significantly in detail and effectiveness depending on the scientist who prepared it.

Once data were transferred, the application specialists (scientists) applied both generalizable and specialty knowledge for each development, often adding their own special techniques or ingredients to create the desired result. Most who were involved in sharing data across geographies and product groups acknowledged that highly creative and innovative processes were very difficult to codify.

MacFadden felt that, although very challenging, data could be effectively collected and disseminated through what he dubbed an "elaborate global knowledge management system." He described the elements of such a system:

It is almost impossible to transfer required knowledge through word of mouth alone, so we need to find some mechanism that puts the information at the fingertips of our technology people and key business decision-makers. For example, consider an applications guy. Suppose his job is to develop a new winning cookie flavor for a particular customer. The objective would be for him to be able to log onto the internal Quest systems, and ask it for 'any ideas for new cookies,' and it would offer him a range of new, innovative ideas for the latest cookie applications developed at other Quest facilities around the world.

It would also give him any information-related activities like manufacturing processes, cost structures, market research regarding the performance of the cookie in various markets, particular ingredients and specific information regarding flavors, as well as subjective and interpretive information provided by the people involved in the cookie's development. It would help him get samples onto his desk within a very short period of time — essentially it would be designed *for* him and *by* him so that it would meet every need he had to do his job well. I want to make it so easy to use and helpful to him that his life rotates around it.

MacFadden felt such a system would provide the Food Division with a huge advantage in the marketplace. He explained:

The creative process of the application specialist is always unique. We cannot capture that 'X' factor — the creative factor in even the most effective knowledge management system — no one can. However, what we hope to do is capture enough knowledge and organize it effectively so that we will not have to 'reinvent the wheel' for every brief.

QUEST'S CRM SYSTEM

An integral part of developing a sustainable competitive advantage was the design and implementation not only of an internal knowledge management system, but of an external system. This was the essence of CRM — allowing customers to tap into Quest's vast global knowledge banks. MacFadden commented on the global aspect of CRM :

Traditionally, the food business has been extremely local and it still is today. What people eat is very much determined by culture. Despite this reality, over the past decade or so, some food companies have become more global. While we deal with a customer base that is increasingly global, we still have to be very sensitive to local customers and country-specific tastes. As a result, we need a strong local face for certain customers.

Being strong locally isn't just limited to whom we use as sales people, but also includes a strong ability to develop flavors and textures for their particular, idiosyncratic needs. This is why a CRM system is so important to us — it will allow us to bring the global knowledge of Quest to local customers.

MacFadden was emphatic that the CRM system he envisioned would go far beyond anything currently at use within Quest.[3] His objective was to design a system that offered customers value-added services that were so rewarding that they would strengthen Quest's position as a preferred supplier. His plan called for the development of a graphical user interface (GUI) through which Quest would share key data with customers. Over time, it was hoped that the GUI could be expanded to allow Quest to also collect data from customers on their processes and product development initiatives. MacFadden believed that these customer databases would eventually allow Quest to facilitate global cooperation between customers; for example, a fully operational CRM could permit Quest to broker a relationship between food manufacturers in Korea and Singapore.

MacFadden explained the rationale behind the development of Quest's CRM:

> Besides getting the infrastructure right (i.e., BPR) I asked myself, 'What else would really differentiate us at the end of the day?' I had this idea that we would have a huge advantage if we had something sitting on customers' desks that was proprietary, and customized.

In addition to strengthening relationships, there were other cost and efficiency advantages promised by CRM. Angel Diaz de Leon, vice-president Business Transformation Processes, commented on one of the drivers of CRM:

> Over the past few years, we have become more and more concerned that our salespeople were spending too much time on non-productive, clerical activities. An internal review we conducted in the U.S. confirmed that too often our salespeople have been spending too much time on non-valuable activities that are conducted away from customers. CRM promises to make our salespeople much more efficient and effective.

The proposed customer interface had a modular design that would allow scalability of end use applications and customer projects within three major product categories — bakery/confectionery, dairy/beverage, and noodles. The CRM system would interface predominantly with the R&D, marketing, and purchasing

---

[3]Within ICI, the term CRM was used quite differently. For example, ICI Paints used CRM to refer to sales force systems that were designed to provide information on customer visits, plans and actions. The CRM definition used by Quest was much broader and included systems to "improve customer relationships."

departments of Quest's customers. Quest would own the equipment and hardware that facilitated the operation of the system, as well as the proprietary software necessary to run it. Some examples of the kinds of resources that would be available to customers included:

- Online project discussion groups
- Industry news and updates
- Scientific databases
- Sample and product ordering
- Online information gathering (i.e., order status and stock availability)

MAJOR STEPS IN ROLLING OUT CRM

It was widely understood that because customer demands were always evolving, CRM would be a continuous work in progress. In February 2000, Boeren envisioned three stages of CRM rollout:

> The first phase would be a one-way Internet site that offered generic information on Quest and our products. This is what we offer now — a Web site, with limited and highly generalized product information, outlining the major categories of businesses Quest pursues globally. Within this first phase we can go further than we currently have by allowing specific customers the option of entering a private area with some proprietary information. However, it would not be interactive.

> The second phase of CRM would involve interaction. The customers would request information specific to their requirements. However, the majority of customer requests would still be facilitated through human interaction.

> The third phase would be full integration. By that I mean that an action by one of our customers would directly result in workflow on our part — eventually, eliminating the human interface.

The specific technological components of Quest's CRM were Boeren's area of responsibility. Boeren outlined four major technological requirements to successfully reach phase three integration. The first requirement was to analyze the compatibility of critical customer data fields. Boeren described this challenge: "What, for instance, Nabisco wants in terms of fields of data in a CRM database may not be identical to what Coca-Cola might want." The second requirement was the gathering and codification of relevant data — on a global basis—from Quest's customers and to a lesser degree from Quest itself. The third and final requirements included testing (creating an internal interface, adding filters, beta-testing), and finally, full roll out to customers.

TIMING AND LOCATION ISSUES

It was believed by most managers associated with BPR that a highly sophisticated CRM system would help create Quest's sustainable competitive advantage. However, where there appeared to be less consensus was over the timing and appropriate speed of the rollout. Senior Quest managers had recently approached MacFadden asking why the process seemed to be moving so slowly, to which he responded:

> We are actually not moving slowly on this; when you consider what needs to be done, it's an immense initiative. Each of the steps of the CRM system is critically inter-dependent and of immense scope.
>
> Take, for example, the responsibility of universally coding internal data, never mind customer specific data. We have to find a very simple way of handling a very complicated process, and we have not yet done this. Even if it offers incredible benefits, our customers will not use our GUI if it is not easy to understand or if they get lost in it.

Others were concerned about CRM being championed out of the Singapore office, as the region was not yet a leader in Internet-based commerce or Web-based alliances. One expatriate manager at Quest with seven years' experience in the region explained:

> E-commerce will be slower in Asia than elsewhere. Our people in Asia who interface with customers don't see many benefits right now. If e-commerce is ever going to work, it's going to have to first be introduced in the U.S. or Europe. These regions should take the lead instead of Asia. Part of the problem is that right now in Asia the cost of trying to get synergies far outweighs the benefits. E-commerce is ultimately based on maximizing efficiencies, which is a big incentive in mature markets but not as big an issue in Asia.
>
> There are still lots of growth opportunities in Asia with the recent up-turn in national economies. We are all very busy and I don't believe it is in our best interest right now to be distracted by e-commerce. This is particularly problematic given weakness in management bench strength in Asia. Less than 10 per cent of our customers in Asia are the kinds of multinational companies that

would most benefit from CRM. Just because we are a global company doesn't mean we don't have lots of local customers.

Other managers were deeply worried about the lack of resources in Quest Asia to complete the task. Betty Tse, regional human resources director, Asia Pacific, for Quest had the following observation:

> In Asia Pacific, within Quest, keeping up with e-commerce and IT requires constant effort. The good news is that in many markets, customer demand for Extranets may not be there. This is a concern because it takes some of the pressure off our people.

UNDER PRESSURE

The challenges of providing CRM leadership were not lost on MacFadden. Prior to Boeren's meeting with International Snackfoods, MacFadden felt that Quest had "between half a year and two years" to implement a CRM system; now he was no longer certain. During their February 28 meeting, Boeren reviewed with MacFadden the details of his recent meeting with Larry Wong at International Snackfoods.

> Wong said that International Snackfoods had recently moved to a regional structure. This means that purchasing was being centralized for the region here in Singapore. Furthermore, I learned that while International Snackfoods had a relatively small sales base in Asia, it was growing at between 40 and 60 per cent per year, which is far faster than many local customers.

> Moreover, I learned that International Snackfoods wants to continue to differentiate between Asian tastes and those from the U.S. and Europe. One example is that Americans continue to prefer flavors that are dairy-based; however, cheese flavors don't do well in Asia. Asians seem to like meat or fish-based flavors. Tastes also vary significantly within Asia. Wong pointed out that while International Snackfoods' BBQ-flavored chips had the same smoky taste in Australia as in the U.S., they had a spicier flavor in Thailand and India. In China, he asserted that end-users prefer a more "meaty" flavor in potato chips. And within a big country like China, he pointed out that tastes vary from region to region. For example, in Northern China consumers seem to want a less salty flavoring than they do in the South.

It was Boeren's impression that International Snackfoods was pushing its suppliers not only to accommodate these local differences in taste, but also to mirror its push toward globalization. To support this view, Boeren again quoted Wong from their earlier meeting:

> It doesn't make sense for International Snackfoods to have global tastes — we cannot import the flavorings — they have to be produced locally. To be cost competitive and to lower lead times and reduce supply volatility, we must localize as much as possible. Therefore, we might as well make products locally flavored. However, it does make sense to globalize our quality standards — chip thickness, freshness guarantees, and the like. Importantly, we also globalize our top brands. Quest's structure must mirror our organization and be globally sophisticated, with local capabilities.
>
> For Quest to be successful, you must be transparent with us. If you want a long-term partnership, both sides must share information. This way we both win. We need trust and transparency. Our businesses are more volatile over here. Our forecasts are often less predictable than in the U.S. or Europe. We need each other's help.
>
> Right now we are in the process of setting up an Extranet with one of your competitors from Germany. The Extranet will allow us to track inventory, order status, and payments. This German supplier is linking up its Hanover facility with our R&D people here in the region.
>
> Other suppliers are also e-mailing us every month to tell us what they are doing around the world for International Snackfoods. They also keep us up-to-date on other generic developments. We don't see this kind of coordinated support from Quest.

MOVING FORWARD

MacFadden wondered how much time he had to respond to International Snackfoods. On the one hand, no one at Quest was comfortable being out-done by a competitor. Furthermore, the world was turning decidedly in favor of CRM linkages. On the other hand, International Snackfoods and other key clients were undergoing their own re-engineering efforts and were not yet strongly demanding CRM. Furthermore, its country-centred approach to product development suggested that linkages to Quest's regional and global technology might be less important to International Snackfoods than having access to strong in-country development teams at Quest. Some argued that it would be smarter for Quest to delay CRM and spend its efforts on building its technology skills in major countries like China, Korea, and Japan.

Despite having a relatively high degree of autonomy in Asia, MacFadden fully realized that any decisions he made would have global consequences — either positively or negatively. His colleague, Antel Dias de Leon, explained:

> Whatever Declan does with International Snackfoods in Singapore will impact what we do in the rest of the world with this customer. We have to assume that International Snackfoods shares information internally. If we open the door to them in Asia, we open the door worldwide. There are consequences beyond Asia in any decision that is made.

Although essentially every customer wanted maximum supplier transparency, responsiveness and information flow, MacFadden was not sure whether this would translate into a willingness to work with Quest in designing and implementing an Extranet. Partly because of this concern, MacFadden wondered whether Quest should focus its first CRM partnership on a global customer in Asia or on an up-and-coming second-tier food company.

Instead of focusing on a large, global account like International Snackfoods, some argued that Quest might be better served by partnering with a more nimble, technology-oriented food company. Evidence from other industries suggested that the greatest benefits came from partnering with tomorrow's industry leaders. However, if MacFadden decided to move in this direction, it was unlikely that Quest would easily find such a partner in Asia. MacFadden commented on the challenge:

> This is Asia and many of Quest's customers do not even have broadband Internet access to facilitate many of the more sophisticated electronic applications we have been discussing. Some of our larger customers in Asia are still using DOS. This is not to say that over the next couple of years they won't upgrade, but currently, their systems are not necessarily state-of-the-art.

Partner selection and roll-out strategy were closely linked. Under one scenario, Quest would implement an internal knowledge management system first, proceed with BPR, and then extend that model externally to its customers. This situation would certainly delay CRM for several years. It would also ensure that the internal systems worked before closely linking with a partner. A delay would also provide time for Asian customers to catch up on technology and help MacFadden better clarify partner selection criteria. MacFadden clearly had some leeway on this matter. Paul Dreschler put the decision in context:

> You have to look at your total business agenda and choose your priorities, make decisions, and allocate resources. There has been a lot of fantastic stuff done, but my question is, does it make money

and will it make money? MacFadden's colleagues all have very different views about what CRM means. Declan has defined it one way but there are different ways of looking at it.

On the downside, MacFadden was deeply aware that in the Internet-era, everything changed overnight. Waiting until everything was internally aligned and everyone was in agreement was highly risky.

Under a second scenario, MacFadden could jump into CRM with a customer who would agree to act as a learning partner. Under this option, Quest would develop a model CRM system based on one strategic partner's needs, and then roll it out to other customers when demanded (but after BPR had progressed more completely). Under this scenario, MacFadden wondered how closely Quest's systems should be aligned with those of its learning partner. Would a more generic system be appropriate at this stage until the optimum level of technological sophistication became clearer? If Quest did develop a more generic CRM model, MacFadden wondered whether it would meet his goal of gaining a sustainable competitive advantage.

MacFadden summarized the reality of the context in which these decisions had to be made:

> These issues are a few of the many priorities I have. On a daily basis, Asia is a region that we need to hold together. I'm not sure if this is the most exciting opportunity Quest faces, or our most terrifying challenge.

The Richard Ivey School of Business gratefully acknowledges the generous support of The Richard and Jean Ivey Fund in the development of this case as part of the RICHARD AND JEAN IVEY FUND ASIAN CASE SERIES.

Exhibit 1

FLAVORS AND FOOD INGREDIENTS: QUEST'S INTEGRATED APPROACH

Dairy Industry

Quest offered a comprehensive range of ingredients and flavors to improve the taste, texture, appearance, shelf-life and overall quality of dairy products, from ice-cream and frozen desserts to cheese and yogurt.

- Starter cultures
- Stabilizers and shelf-life extenders
- Whipping proteins
- Emulsifiers
- Natural and artificial flavors

Beverages

Quest flavors and ingredients enhanced beverages from soft drinks, teas and herbals to distilled spirits, beers, wines and cordials.

- Natural flavors
- Stabilizers
- Artificial flavors
- Vanilla extract
- Enzymes

Bakery and Confectionery Products

Quest technology improved the market appeal of bakery and confectionery products, from breads, cakes and crackers to candy and chewing gum.

- Heat-stable, natural and fat flavors
- Vanilla extract
- Fat replacement systems
- Shelf-life extenders
- Enzymes
- Cultures
- Emulsifiers
- Proteins

Exhibit 1 (continued)

Meals, Soups, Sauces and Dressings

Quest ingredients and flavors gave sauces, gravies, prepared meals, dressings, soups and related products characteristics consumers preferred:
- Natural flavors
- Replacement ingredients
- Meat flavors
- Tenderizers
- Emulsifiers
- Dried vegetables
- MSG replacers
- Yeast extracts
- Stabilizers
- Cultures

Snack Foods

Specialty snack foods benefited from Quest's distinctive flavors, spices and ingredient blends.
- Cheese flavors
- Cheese "plus" flavors
- Beef flavors
- Chicken flavors
- Seafood flavors
- Specialty blends

Meat Industry

Quest ingredients helped create the quality difference in meat products, from fermented items like pepperoni, to hams and meat spreads.
- Cultures
- Shelf extenders
- Carrageenans
- Enzyme tenderizers
- Flavors
  - Autolysed yeast
  - Hydrolysed vegetable proteins
  - Low fat flavors
  - Replacement flavors

Exhibit 1 (continued)

Human Nutrition

Quest supplied specialized ingredients to supplement the nutritional value of products including functional foods/drinks, supplements, infant formula, enriched sports drinks and clinical foods.

- Lactose

Cell Nutrition

Proteins, hydrolysates (Peptones) and yeast extracts, for use in culturing micro-organisms, and laboratory and industrial fermentations (which provided essential peptides, amino acids, vitamins and minerals, as well as a complex mixture of yeast cell-wall derived carbohydrates).

Harvard Business Review

www.hbr.org

How can Reboredo foster creativity in her current employees and nurture creative individuals who join the company in the future?

What's Stifling the Creativity at CoolBurst?

by Suzy Wetlaufer

Reprint 97511X

With the competition getting hot, a beverage company must learn how to fire up its creative juices.

HBR CASE STUDY

What's Stifling the Creativity at CoolBurst?

by Suzy Wetlaufer

Luisa Reboredo had never been one to count her hours in the office, let alone take all the vacation days she had accumulated in her 15 years with CoolBurst, a Miami-based fruit-juice company. Now, as the newly appointed CEO, she seemed to live at work. The job exhilarated her, and she had big plans for the company's future—if she could just get performance on track first.

It took a great deal of pleading, therefore, for Reboredo's 18-year-old son, Alfonse, to get her to attend Miami's popular outdoor art festival with him one Saturday in May. She had regularly been working weekends, using the time to pore over CoolBurst's books in an effort to figure out why annual revenues were stuck at $30 million and why profits hadn't risen for four years straight.

Finally, the two struck a deal: Luisa would attend the art festival in the morning and spend the rest of the day at the office.

They arrived at 10, and already the sun was baking the festival grounds. Alfonse, almost a full foot taller than Luisa and a basketball star at Southwest Miami High, put his arm around his mother. "Mom, this is great—you've got to get out more often," he practically sang. "You're missing the action stuck inside that office."

Luisa sighed. Raising Alfonse by herself hadn't been easy, and now that she had reached the top of her career and could comfortably afford his college tuition, the last thing she wanted was to have the company she'd helped to build collapse beneath her. Just the thought of CoolBurst's stagnant performance suddenly made her tense. Why was it, she wondered, that CoolBurst wasn't growing anymore? For over a decade, it had been the most successful juice maker in the Southeast. Practically every school in Florida, Georgia, Alabama, and South Carolina had a CoolBurst vending machine in its cafeteria, and thousands of restaurants listed

---

HBR's cases, which are fictional, present common managerial dilemmas.

Jenkins and Velez presented their new drinks to LaRoue, only to be shouted out of his office

Suzy Wetlaufer is a senior editor at HBR.

CoolBurst's apple, grape, and cranberry drinks by brand name on their menus. In fact, CoolBurst had grown so steadily over the years that its parent company, a Chicago-based conglomerate, rarely interfered with operations. Lately, however, Luisa had been receiving weekly phone calls from the higher-ups in Chicago inquiring about budget projections, expenses, and personnel changes.

"Mom, stop thinking about work!" Alfonse shouted, interrupting Luisa's thoughts. "You should see the expression on your face!"

Luisa tried to smile but shrugged instead. "I'm sorry, Alfonse," she said. "Let's look around."

Her son readily agreed, steering her toward a row of paintings by a local artist they both liked. Then Alfonse stopped for a moment. "Wait a second, Mom," he said, "let me grab a drink first. I'm burning up."

Alfonse dashed over to a man selling drinks from a cart a few yards away. The cart was topped by a large red umbrella emblazoned with the words Destroy Your Thirst! Drink a Thirst Smasher. A moment later, he was back, unscrewing the cap of a red glass bottle shaped like a rocket.

"Alfonse!" Luisa practically gasped. "How could you?"

"How could I what?" Alfonse replied, somewhat irritated. "I couldn't get a CoolBurst around here if I tried, Mom. I suppose I could sprint over to the high school, but that wouldn't exactly be convenient.

"Besides," Alfonse added, "everyone knows CoolBurst is for kids. These Thirst Smashers are something new. Get a load of this flavor—Mango Tango. It tastes fabulous."

Luisa cringed—she knew all about Mango Tango. In fact, the flavor had been invented in CoolBurst's own labs, a collaboration between chief scientist Carol Velez and CoolBurst's then marketing director, Sam Jenkins. The two had concocted Mango Tango and four other exotic drinks on the sly about a year earlier. But when they presented them to the company's then CEO, Garth LaRoue, he had been so angry about their unauthorized use of time that he had practically fired them both. Velez hadn't had her heart in her job since. And Jenkins had left CoolBurst shortly thereafter to join Thirst Smashers, one of a half dozen start-ups that had recently begun venturing into the drink business in the Southeast. To Luisa, it felt

as if every month a new company joined the competitive fray, each one coming from a different angle. Thirst Smashers was parking its drink carts on every corner. Drink-Ups, another new player, was selling carbonated juice drinks and advertising like mad on the radio with a jingle even she couldn't get out of her head.

But so far, Luisa reminded herself, none of the start-ups had put a noticeable dent in CoolBurst's market share in schools and restaurants. The reason, she figured, was the company's efficient set of systems, in both the factory and the field. CoolBurst's purchasing agents and plant operations were located in Atlanta, where managers worked to make a high-quality product as inexpensively as possible. The company's salespeople were all over the Southeast, developing close relationships with their customers. An advanced—and pricey—information technology system, which CoolBurst had installed in 1990, allowed salespeople in the field to place orders, which were filled swiftly by a fleet of CoolBurst drivers. And finally, the company's labs were located at headquarters, where Velez and a small staff focused on improving the flavors of CoolBurst's products and the efficiency of the company's factory processes.

CoolBurst is like a well-oiled machine, Luisa told herself: not many bells and whistles to what we do, but we do it well. Perhaps that was why it caused such a scandal when Velez and Jenkins got together to invent Mango Tango and the other new flavors. Everyone in the company was sick and tired of the way Jenkins was trying to change things. Most employees considered him a troublemaker—a transplanted New Yorker and business school graduate who did nothing but harangue people to "think outside the box."

"What box is he talking about?" was the refrain from most of CoolBurst's 200 employees, who were predominantly native Miamians who had joined the company after high school or college. CoolBurst had been an independent company until 1975, and it still retained much of its old organizational culture, which reflected the traditional, family-oriented background of its Cuban-born founder.

Employees were loyal and conservative in both mind and manner. The company's dress code was formal, even in Miami's warm climate, and employees treated one another with a politeness that seemed like a throwback to the 1950s. But as old-fashioned as it seemed, that politeness was an aspect of CoolBurst's culture that employees valued highly. No one at CoolBurst argued. No one swore. No one complained that the company's offices were small and nondescript. No one ever answered the phone in any way other than the expected "Thank you for calling CoolBurst. How may I be of service?" The company was a calm and civilized place to work in the midst of a changing, chaotic world.

It's no wonder, then, Luisa thought, that Sam Jenkins rubbed a lot of people the wrong way: he was always confronting colleagues about their assumptions and ways of doing business. His favorite phrase was "Everyone's entitled to my opinion." And he seemed to delight in challenging rules and norms around the office. He often arrived late to work, left early, and blared rock-and-roll music from his computer's CD-ROM drive. Some days, when he left at lunchtime, he would tape a note to his door that read, "Gone to the movies to get my creative juices flowing. Ha!" Even his office space seemed to challenge the status quo. The walls were covered with large, haunting photographs he had taken while traveling through Africa and India, and several fanciful "dream catchers" hung from the ceiling. When the phone rang, Jenkins always answered, "Yeah?"

Worse, his behavior had a negative effect on the productivity of other employees. When Jenkins left early, other people followed. If the director of marketing worked half days, they figured, why couldn't they? As a result, the phones in customer service often went unanswered.

Jenkins's work habits seemed to suit him: despite his odd hours, he always got a lot done. But Luisa—and many others in top management—had noticed that allowing other employees this freedom didn't seem to do much for the overall output of the company.

Luisa liked Jenkins. She knew he had passed up high-paying offers in consulting and on Wall Street to take the job at CoolBurst because, as he put it, he loved business "in the trenches." She also knew that, soon after starting at CoolBurst, Jenkins had quickly grown worried about the company. He told everyone who would listen that CoolBurst's past success had been a simple matter of being in the right place at the right time—and a fortuitous lack of competition. "The bubble is going to burst

one of these days," he kept repeating. Cool-Burst had to innovate, he warned—or it would evaporate.

Jenkins wanted to lead the charge. First, he started working on the director of distribution, Roger Blatt. Why was it, he asked, that CoolBurst was sold only in school vending machines and in restaurants? What about opening up new channels? How about handing out CoolBursts to everyone who stepped off a plane at Miami International Airport? Blatt nearly roared when he heard that suggestion. There were a hundred reasons why that couldn't be done. For one, the airport had extremely tight security regulations. And where would the drivers park? How could they possibly get the juice to the gates? And what about keeping it cold? Finance certainly wouldn't approve the idea anyway.

Blatt's final words on the matter were strong: "If it ain't broke, don't fix it."

For a while after his run-in with distribution, Jenkins restricted his creativity campaign to his own territory. His first idea was to get CoolBurst—or maybe even its corporate parent—to cough up some money for advertising. Sure, CoolBurst had advertised in the past, but minimally, and never on TV. In fact, all advertising had been designed in-house and usually consisted of point-of-purchase posters. Jenkins had a different plan in mind. Cool-Burst needed fresh minds from outside the company to help create a new vision of the brand. After making his case for three months, he was given a modest budget. He immediately hired a New York firm well known for its jazzy TV commercials.

But the agency didn't last long at Cool-Burst. In their first meeting with CoolBurst's management team, the account executives launched into what they called a "creativity-enhancement exercise." After dimming the lights, they urged the CoolBurst managers to close their eyes and imagine themselves on a desert island, dying of thirst. "Suddenly, an angel arrives and offers you the drink of your dreams. Let your imagination go—you can have anything you want—no constraints," incanted one ad executive. "Let yourself fantasize."

"That's enough!" snapped LaRoue, who was still CEO at the time. "I'm all for new ideas around here, but these kinds of mind games are a waste of time. Either you're born creative or you're not. Fantasizing about an angel isn't going to do us a bit of good. We all should be back at our desks working."

LaRoue's comments hadn't surprised Luisa. He was nearing 65 and had been at Cool-Burst his entire career, starting as a stock boy in the factory. He valued tradition, just as he valued self-discipline and respect for authority. He had quickly come to distrust Jenkins, and, after the incident with the advertising agency, he had strongly urged Luisa to get rid of him.

Even if she had wanted to, Luisa didn't have the chance. A few days later, Jenkins and Velez presented their four new drinks to LaRoue, only to be shouted out of his office. When Luisa found Velez back in the lab later, she was dejectedly pouring the prototypes down the drain. Luisa stopped her before she emptied the Mango Tango, and took a taste. It was delicious, and she told her so.

"It doesn't make any difference that it's delicious," said Velez. "You can't do anything different in this company. Everyone gets hysterical."

"Well, I won't get hysterical," Luisa said, "and I may soon have the final say as the new CEO."

"Forget it," said Velez. "That's not what CoolBurst is about. We're not a creative company. We're just a little juice company that knows how to do one thing well—make plain old juice and deliver it to plain old schools and restaurants." She looked Luisa straight in the eye. "We've got one creative person here, and he makes everyone nervous. Even if you told everyone it was okay to be creative like Sam Jenkins, no one would know what to do. How do you make a bunch of people who are happy doing the same old thing come up with new ideas? It's just not the CoolBurst way."

Velez's assertion didn't make Luisa happy, but it couldn't be denied. CoolBurst wasn't a creative place, and it didn't attract creative people—with the exception of Jenkins and Velez. And when it did find that rare creative person who wanted to make a difference, management didn't know what to do with him—apart from forcing him out the door.

As Luisa stood outside in the blazing sun with Alfonse—who was polishing off his Mango Tango Thirst Smasher—she couldn't stop thinking about Velez's assessment of Cool-Burst. Was the company really a lost cause when it came to the issue of creativity? Were its employees really as stolid as Velez thought they were? And was there some way to get everyone—from distribution to manufacturing—to think of new and exciting ways to revitalize CoolBurst's product line and way of doing business?

Was there a way, Luisa wondered, to make CoolBurst a more welcoming, nurturing place for creative individuals like Jenkins? Sure, some of his ideas were off the wall; Luisa smiled to herself as she remembered his plan to have thousands of bottles of CoolBurst wash up on the Miami beaches during spring break. But others, such as exotic new flavors, were terrific.

"Hey, Mom, you're still thinking about work!" Alfonse broke into Luisa's thoughts once more. "Let's have some fun. Let me buy you a Mango Tango!"

How can Reboredo foster creativity in her current employees and nurture creative individuals who join the company in the future?

Reprint 97511X
To order, call 800-988-0886
or 617-783-7500 or go to www.hbr.org

Harvard Business Review

www.hbr.org

U.S. and Canada
800-988-0886
617-783-7500
617-783-7555 fax

THE LATEST CONSUMERS YOU NEED TO GET TO KNOW: Influencers from the Pages of 'Karma Queens, Geek Gods and Innerpreneurs'. (News)

Advertising Age July 23 , 2007

Byline: Matt Kinsey

mkinsey@adage.com

The consumer has a new face-again.

Yet another wave of millennial consumer taxonomy is headed down the pike. Where once the terms "soccer mom" and "metrosexual" were enough for marketers to target stay-at-home matriarchs and young, urban males, a rise in new media and more-fluid career paths have led researchers to uncover new consumer targets. These influencers maintain a wider range of media behaviors, possess a higher degree of market smarts and attitude, and are highly skilled at spreading the word.

Consumer Eyes, a New York-based marketing firm, recently released its first collection of data on the subject in a book titled "Karma Queens, Geek Gods and Innerpreneurs." After culling thousands of brand insights—S.C. Johnson & Son, Motorola, PepsiCo, and P&G are on its client roster—using the consultancy's Consumer Immersion process, founder Ron Rentel and his team selected nine C-Types of true-to-life consumers who they believe should be on every marketer's radar.

The resulting profiles may sound like stylized caricatures, but they're personas with tangible auto, wardrobe and mixed-media preferences, the company said. And while the book notes C-Types are not a "black box to success," Consumer Eyes hopes its research sparks creativity in marketing innovation.

Here's a handy guide to the nine new influencers. Along with some suggestions from Consumer Eyes, we've matched each character with a better-known celebrity counterpart. Just to give, you know, the bigger picture.

WHAT'S YOUR C-TYPE?

Forget soccer moms and metrosexuals. Here are nine influencers identified by New York marketing firm Consumer Eyes—along with their celebrity counterparts. Find out why Ron Rentel and Co. think these consumers should be on marketers' radars.

KARMA QUEENS

Typically in her 40s or 50s, the Karma Queen is best described as a baby boomer ex-hippie. She appreciates woman-to-woman brand connections, and pays attention to mind-body-spirit marketing trifectas. She also tends to drive quirky, streamlined autos (VW bug, Honda Element).

DENIM DADS

The modern stay-at-home dad is admired for seeking work-life balance. He spends a good chunk of his day online, gleaning parenting tips off Slowlane.com and posting his own. He shares musical tastes with his kids, and appreciates the changing tables in the men's room at Home Depot.

PARENTOCRATS

Parentocrats obsess over the best for their children-at any cost. They buy products that multitask as well as they do and invest in spy software such as Net Nanny. Their lives stay organized with Mom's Family Calendar, a hit on Amazon.

MS. INDEPENDENTS

With loads of disposable income and no one to spend it on but herself, this single woman is a believer in "power purchases" such as high-end designer clothing. And she's as much a force at home as she is in the workplace, tuning in to DIY Network and reading *Blueprint* magazine.

INNERPRENEURS

Innerpreneurs of all ages and genders are the brainstormers whose plans to change their own lives end up changing ours. They like brands to get involved, not just donate to a cause. Even their time off is hardly a vacation: They're likely to take trips co-sponsored by Globe Aware or the Sierra Club.

MIDDLEMEN

A seemingly hopeless but content 21- to 35-year-old, the Middleman is uninterested in giving up his laid-back lifestyle, working jobs with no promise of advancement. For some marketers, though, he's a catch: He's the backbone of the fast-food industry and is a passionate gamer.

CULTURE CROSSERS

Culture Crossers are defined by who they choose to be vs. what they're born into. Their transcontinental tastes are reflected in fashion: keffiyehs (Arabic scarves) and

Bathing Ape T-shirts popular in Tokyo. They attend concerts by the likes of Bjork, skim *Anthem* and *Trace* magazines and check in with Flavorpill.

GEEK GODS

The Geek God, 20 to 35, can be summoned via Geeks on Call. He's short on neither disposable income nor free time, spending hours on Gizmodo and Engadget. Count on him for loyalty and buzz, but beware: He'll call you out on your missteps.

E-litists

They're what *The New York Times* describes as "light green" Cost for these folks is not the bottom line; they enjoy the status and bragging rights. E-litists decorate with low-VOC paints and clean with Method products. These couples shop at Whole Foods Market and listen to NPR in their Toyota Prius.

Harvard Business Review ⚜

www.hbr.org

The psychographic profiling that passes for market segmentation these days is a mostly wasteful diversion from its original and true purpose—discovering customers whose behavior can be changed or whose needs are not being met.

Rediscovering Market Segmentation

by Daniel Yankelovich and David Meer

Reprint R0602G

The psychographic profiling that passes for market segmentation these days is a mostly wasteful diversion from its original and true purpose—discovering customers whose behavior can be changed or whose needs are not being met.

Rediscovering Market Segmentation

by Daniel Yankelovich and David Meer

There are many different kinds of people, and they display about as many different buying patterns. That simple truth is well understood by those responsible for market research, product development, pricing, sales, and strategy. But they haven't been getting much help from a venerable technique—market segmentation—which, if properly applied, would guide companies in tailoring their product and service offerings to the groups most likely to purchase them. Instead, market segmentation has become narrowly focused on the needs of advertising, which it serves mainly by populating commercials with characters that viewers can identify with—the marketing equivalent of central casting.

This is hardly the state of affairs we anticipated 40 years ago when one of us introduced the concept of nondemographic segmentation in HBR as a corrective to the narrow reliance on purely demographic ways of grouping consumers. In 1964, in "New Criteria for Market Segmentation," Daniel Yankelovich asserted that:

• Traditional demographic traits such as age, sex, education levels, and income no longer said enough to serve as a basis for marketing strategy.

• Nondemographic traits such as values, tastes, and preferences were more likely to influence consumers' purchases than their demographic traits were.

• Sound marketing strategy depended on identifying segments that were potentially receptive to a particular brand and product category.

The idea was to broaden the use of segmentation so that it could inform not just advertising but also product innovation, pricing, choice of distribution channels, and the like. Yet today's segmentations do very little of this, even though markets and media are, if anything, even more fragmented today than they were in 1964 and consumers even more diverse and accustomed to following their own tastes and impulses.

Segmentation can do vastly more than serve as a source of human types, which individually go by such colorful monikers as High-Tech Harry and Joe Six-Pack and are known collectively by the term "psychographics." Psychographics may capture some truth about real people's lifestyles, attitudes, self-image, and aspirations, but it is very weak at predicting what any of these people is likely to purchase in any given product category. It thus happens to be very poor at giving corporate decision makers any idea of how to keep the customers they have or gain new ones.

The failings of psychographics, however, and the disappointments it has produced in its users, should not cast doubt on the validity of careful segmentation overall. Indeed, marketers continue to rely on it, and line executives increasingly demand segmentations that the whole enterprise can put into action. Because of the technique's underlying validity, and managers' continuing need for what it can do, there's good reason to think that segmentation's drift from its original purpose and potency can be halted. Good segmentations identify the groups most worth pursuing—the underserved, the dissatisfied, and those likely to make a first-time purchase, for example. They are dynamic—they recognize that the first-time purchaser may become underserved or dissatisfied if his or her situation changes. And they tell companies what products to place before the most susceptible consumers.

In this article, we'll describe the elements of a smart segmentation strategy. We'll explain how segmentations meant to strengthen brand identity and make an emotional connection with consumers differ from those capable of telling a company which markets it should enter and what goods to make. And we'll introduce a tool we call the "gravity of decision spectrum," which focuses on the form of consumer behavior that should be of greatest interest to marketers—the relationship of consumers to a product or product category, not to their jobs, their friends, their family, or their community, all of which lay in the realm of psychographics.

The Drift into Nebulousness
The years after World War II were marked by extraordinary innovations in consumer products—transistor radios, disposable diapers, razor cartridges, pleasant-tasting sugarless colas, among them. For products so groundbreaking and widely desired, advertising did not have to do much more than announce their existence and describe their dazzling features.

By the early 1960s, however, consumers were becoming less predictable in their buying habits: Many people without much education had become affluent; others with sophisticated tastes had become very price conscious. As a result, tastes and purchasing patterns no longer neatly aligned with age and income, and purely demographic segmentations lost their ability to guide companies' decisions.

As time went on, product introductions remained frequent, but they increasingly amounted to refinements of existing offerings that had originally answered real consumer needs but now merely catered to mild preferences. With ever more trivial improvements to report on, and few ways to distinguish a client's product from the competition's, advertising grew boring and bored with itself. Gradually, the focus of creative departments shifted from the product to the consumer: If, by the 1970s, products had become less distinctive, people seemed to be bursting with unprecedented variety.

One way companies found to convince particular groups of consumers that a product was perfect for them was to place in the advertising message a person whom they resembled or wished they did. Another way, which followed from the consumer orientation of the first, was to emphasize the emotional rather than the functional benefits products offered—pride of ownership, increased status, sex appeal. Cake mixes to which a fresh egg had to be added, for example, may have tasted no better than earlier versions containing powdered egg. But they sold well because the extra step allowed the preparer to feel she was fulfilling a wife's traditional domestic role. In contrast to breakthrough products—such as an effective over-the-counter dandruff shampoo—that addressed intense unmet needs, ordinary third-generation products had to find customers who were already and especially susceptible to their allure. Since the attraction was based on things like status, it made sense to fashion segments reflecting the personal characteristics and lifestyles of the target consumers. As competitors increased the speed and skill with which they could copy or reengineer products, the functional dimension of existing offerings became less compelling. Ironically, by the mid-1970s, belief in the power of imagery to stimulate sales of dull items may have begun to take pressure off product developers to come up

Daniel Yankelovich is chairman of Viewpoint Learning, a firm that promotes problem solving through dialogue, and DYG, a market research firm that tracks social trends. He is based in San Diego. **David Meer** (dmeer@marakon.com) is a partner in the New York office of Marakon Associates, an international strategy consulting firm.

with products and services displaying genuinely innovative technology and fresh design, thus aggravating the problem.

Two concurrent developments gave this new emphasis on the consumer's self-conception, emotions, and personality an extra measure of rigor. Social scientists began to apply their modes of analysis to business problems, and business executives, confused by the fragmentation of the mass audience and the speed with which tastes were changing, welcomed their insights. Using attitudinal indicators similar to those elicited by personality tests, psychologists carved out marketing segments based on their members' shared worldview. Those early segments were populated with the Inner-Directed, Traditionalists, Hedonists, and the like.

In 1978, Arnold Mitchell and his colleagues at the Stanford Research Institute launched the Values and Lifestyles (VALS) program, a commercial research service, which was soon retained by scores of consumer product companies and advertising agencies. VALS drew heavily on frameworks developed by Harvard sociologist David Riesman, coauthor of *The Lonely Crowd,* and Brandeis psychologist Abraham Maslow, who posited the now well-known hierarchy of needs. VALS classified individuals according to nine enduring psychological types. An individual consumer's behavior, the theory went, could in turn be explained by his or her correspondence to one of those types. VALS and similar models soon turned psychographics into the most accepted mode of segmentation. Not surprisingly, it was embraced by advertising departments and agencies, which appreciated a certifiably scientific technique whose stock-in-trade was inventing characters, just as they themselves had been doing for some time.

Psychographics, it should be said, proved to be effective at brand reinforcement and positioning. The Pepsi Generation campaign of decades ago, for example, did coalesce a wide assortment of consumers into a group that identified with the youth culture emerging at the time. But even though campaigns built on psychographics are good at moving viewers emotionally, the characteristics and attitudes that such ads invoke are simply not the drivers of commercial activity. Those tend to be things

Different Segmentations for Different Purposes

Psychographic segmentations can be used to create advertising that will influence consumers to think warmly about a particular brand. But they're not as well suited for other purposes. You would need a different kind of nondemographic segmentation to investigate, for instance, what kinds of products to make. Here we set out the different characteristics of these two types of segmentation exercises.

	Segmentations to develop advertising	Segmentations to develop new products
Populations studied	Users of the product or service to be advertised	Users of related products or services that already meet similar needs; partners such as distributors and retailers
Data sources tapped	Attitude surveys	Purchase and usage data on consumers, supplemented by surveys; analyses of consumers' finances and channel preferences
Analytical tools used	Statistical analysis of survey results	Analysis of customers (both in the field and in the laboratory) who remain loyal and those who switch to competing offerings
Outputs	Segments that differ in their responses to a given message	Segments that differ in their purchasing power, goals, aspirations, and behavior

like purchasing history, product loyalty, and a propensity to trade up, all of which are informed by attitudes and values that lead consumers to view particular offerings differently. What's more, psychographic segmentations have done little to enlighten the companies that commission them about which markets to enter or what kinds of offers to make, how products should be taken to market, and how they should be priced.

Despite its disappointing performance, market segmentation is still widely used. In 2004, for example, when Marakon Associates and the Economist Intelligence Unit surveyed 200 senior executives of large companies, 59% of them reported that they had conducted a major segmentation exercise during the previous two years. Yet the evidence suggests it's not a very effective tool: Only 14% of the executives said they derived real value from the exercise.

What happens when a company attempts to apply a segmentation appropriate for developing ad campaigns to product development or pricing decisions? Consider the experience of a company we'll call HomeAirCo, a leading manufacturer and installer of home heating and cooling systems. The chief marketing officer, after less than a year in that position, commissioned a respected consumer research company skilled in statistical analysis to conduct an expensive segmentation study with input from HomeAirCo's advertising agency. The agency was able to create an entertaining campaign featuring characters based on five typologies faithfully reflecting the interests and viewing habits of the members of each segment. One, for example, portrayed a Traditionalist male trying to work on his own heating system and botching it while his wife nagged him to call HomeAirCo; another showed a woman doing yoga in an ideal environment because she had a HomeAirCo system. But every segment had the same number of HomeAirCo customers in it, leaving the firm at a loss to know which groups would be most likely to want to upgrade their temperature control systems. The segmentation's many oversights included a failure to identify buyers of older homes in affluent neighborhoods who, the firm's own anecdotal experience suggested, would probably be the most likely purchasers of such a system.

The fact is that even the most memorable advertising, if based on a crudely drawn seg-

The Miller Lite ads featuring mud-wrestling supermodels certainly impressed the young, male segment they were intended to reach, but sales did not increase.

mentation, will do little to spur sales or garner market share. The recent "Catfight" campaign for Miller Lite, for example, featuring mud-wrestling supermodels, certainly made an impression on the young, male segment it was intended to reach, but sales of that brand of beer did not increase. As it happens, there is a segment of light-beer drinkers that would gravitate to Miller Lite if only its members knew it had fewer carbohydrates than Bud Light. How do we know? A Miller campaign that told them so did indeed increase sales.

The Way Back

If meaningful segmentations depend on finding patterns in your customers' actual buying behavior, then to construct one properly, you need to gather the relevant data. Depending on the question your exercise is ultimately aimed at answering, you would want information about, say, which benefits and features matter to your customers. Or which customers are willing to pay higher prices or demand lower ones. Or the relative advantages and disadvantages customers identify in your existing offerings. You'll also need data on emerging social, economic, and technological trends that may alter purchasing and usage patterns.

Many companies capture this information routinely. If yours does not, you can use qualitative research to explore underlying motives and needs propelling current purchases and use quantitative research to understand competitive strengths and vulnerabilities. You can reexamine the sales data you already have to reveal the hidden patterns in customers' behavior. And you can retain trend-tracking services.

Armed with such data, you can then fashion segments that are both revealing and applicable. Such segments will:
- Reflect the company's strategy;
- Indicate where sources of revenue or profit may lie;
- Identify consumers' values, attitudes, and beliefs as they relate specifically to product or service offerings;
- Focus on actual customer behavior;
- Make sense to top executives;
- Accommodate or anticipate changes in markets or consumer behavior.

Let's consider each aspect in turn.

What are we trying to do? When companies change marketing chiefs, a new segmentation is rarely far behind. The new CMO often uses a segmentation exercise as a way to put his or her stamp on the business. Unfortunately, few marketing chiefs know or have thought about which of their company's strategic decisions would benefit from the guidance of a segmentation. For a traditional brokerage house, for instance, the main strategic challenge might be how to reduce customer defections to discount brokers. For a personal-care products company, it might be how to extend a strong soap brand into deodorants. And for a fast-food chain, it might be whether to come up with healthier menu alternatives. Segmentations designed to shed light on these questions won't try to explore the personalities of customers; they will try to identify groups of potentially interested or susceptible customers sufficiently numerous and lucrative to justify pursuit. Subsequent strategic moves will, of course, call for new and different segmentations.

Which customers drive profits? To be valid, a segmentation must identify groups that matter to a company's financial performance. To start, companies can rank their own customers by profitability so as to concentrate the right amount of attention on them. But to grow revenues, a company should understand what makes its best customers as profitable as they are and then seek new customers who share at least a couple of those characteristics. For instance, a luggage company whose soft but durable carry-on bags earn its highest margins might notice that the majority of the people who buy the bags are international flyers. It would therefore pursue other international travelers as potential customers.

To understand how important this question is, consider the experience of one leading bank with a large wealth management business. The bank had become concerned that its overall business was suffering from low rates of growth and a stagnant market share. Its existing segmentation sorted customers according to the level of employee that served them—relationship manager, senior branch personnel, or junior branch personnel—which mostly depended on customer assets and income. Relationship managers had the most profitable customers, and so forth. However, the bank knew next to nothing about what might distinguish one relationship-manager customer from another.

The bank decided to go beyond what it knew about its existing customer base and acquire market research on the lifetime value of wealthy prospects. The research was of three types:

• Demographic (age, occupation, assets, and so on);

• Behavioral (which services customers already used, how many institutions they did business with, how many transactions they made in a month);

• Attitudinal (financial sophistication, time spent on investments, risk tolerance).

The segmentation that resulted differed markedly from its predecessor. Every component of the three broad drivers of profitability contributed to an understanding of lifetime value. For instance, the new segments identified, such as Young Families, revealed high variations in profitability even in the existing high-profit segment. Equipped with this information, the bank was more willing to embark on the expensive task of tailoring offerings to potential clients, since it had greater confidence that the effort would turn out to be economically worthwhile. Three segments it discovered—On Their Way, Established Families, and Retirement Planners—contributed almost no profit, even though they accounted for half the customer base. Yet many of the individuals who fell into those segments had been assigned to relationship managers. The bank acted quickly to reduce the cost of servicing those people by reassigning them to more junior branch personnel, to call centers, or to the Web.

Which attitudes matter to the buying decision? Even though segmenting customers according to immutable personality traits rarely bears much fruit, there is a place for examining people's lifestyles, attitudes, self-image, and aspirations. They should be explored, as the bank did, in a context that is directly related to the product or service under study. Unlike purely psychographic segments, these characteristics can be expected to change along with the customers' values and environment.

What are my customers actually doing? While relevant attitudes, values, and expressed preferences can bring color and insight to a segmentation, they lack the predictive power of actual purchase behavior, such as heaviness of use, brand switching, and retail-format or channel selection. If you want to understand how a consumer would respond to products or features that have not yet been introduced, you can elicit the next best thing to actual behavior by creating laboratory simulations to which special analytic techniques can be applied. One of them, called "conjoint analysis," involves presenting consumers with combinations of features. It then asks the consumers how willing they would be to purchase the product in question if particular attributes were added or removed, or if the price changed.

Here's an example of how it works: A pet food manufacturer gave consumers an opportunity to design their ideal pet food container. The consumers in the test saw on their computer screens a generic package to which they could drag and drop features they valued, such as a resealable opening and a handle attached to the 25-pound size. They were next asked how much more they would pay for products containing different combinations of such features. The consumers were then segmented according to their degree of price sensitivity and desire for convenience. On this basis, the company could redesign its packaging with added features that would maintain existing customers and attract new ones. It could also jettison features whose cost would have required charging too high an overall price.

Will this segmentation make sense to senior management? Modern marketing practitioners view their field as outward facing—that is, focused on listening and communicating to consumers and markets. In fact, marketing may do itself harm by failing to make itself understood by its internal constituency: senior management. As marketing has become more scientific and specialized, its practitioners have increasingly turned to advanced statistical techniques for dissecting segments into ever finer slices containing improbable combinations of traits. The masters of these techniques are often tempted to flaunt their technical virtuosity instead of defining segments that make intuitive sense to senior managers. If the segments seem inconsistent with managers' long experience, and managers cannot grasp how they were derived, the research they yield is unlikely to be accepted and applied.

One financial services company found this out the hard way. The firm, which develops investment products sold by third-party investment advisers, wanted a bigger role for itself in asset management, a service usually

confined to wealthy investors. So it created a full-service offering designed to accommodate smaller investors. The challenge the company faced was to find out which kinds of advisers would be most likely to recommend the service to this new category of clients. Unfortunately, the advisers' existing classifications—national broker/dealer, regional broker/dealer, bank officer, and independent—revealed differences in recommendation patterns too minor to be meaningful.

The company therefore decided to segment its investment advisers in a more meaningful way—according to the kinds of recommendations they made to their clients. At first, the firm took an approach that was statistically powerful but highly complex. It developed profiles of typical investors based on their age, assets, risk tolerance, and the like. Then in a survey it asked the advisers to select a mix of investments suited to each customer profile. The statistical analysis teased out the underlying investment style of each adviser and then grouped together those with like patterns. Some advisers, for example, rarely recommended individually traded stocks, while others made stocks the foundation of their clients' portfolios.

Although the segmentation was mathematically sound, management did not trust its findings. For one thing, the segmentation relied heavily on whether advisers received fees or commissions, a distinction the statistical analysis determined was important. Since the new product was to be fee based, however, the commission-based segments would be largely irrelevant. So the senior managers could not understand why a segmentation along those lines had been made. Perhaps they would have accepted the study if they had been able to understand how its conclusions had been reached. But the study's reliance on esoteric statistical procedures foreclosed that possibility. If nothing else, the managers charged with applying the study's findings worried that they would lack answers for top management in the event the segmentation failed.

The in-house marketing science team and the consulting firm assisting it decided to recast the segmentation using simple criteria, not statistics. First, the advisers were grouped on the basis of the average net worth of their clients. And then they were grouped according to whether their clients' investments were actively managed. The result was four segments rated on two dimensions. We list them here by internal title in descending order of client wealth and portfolio activity.

- Active Investors (high-net-worth clients, strong reliance on actively managed investments such as stocks and bonds);
- Upscale Coaches (high-net-worth clients, little reliance on actively managed investments);
- Mass-Market Coaches (low-net-worth clients, strong reliance on actively managed investments);
- Product-Oriented (low-net-worth clients, little reliance on actively managed investments).

The Upscale Coaches, it turned out, were the most liable to consider the new asset-management product. The Mass-Market Coaches also showed some potential. The segments bracketing those two had almost no potential. In subsequent interviews, the Active Investors confessed they viewed the company developing the new product as a competitor offering a service uncomfortably close to their own. The Product-Oriented segment had the opposite objection: Their clients were not interested in having anyone actively manage their assets. But the new product could complement the service that the two middle groups provided without threatening to replace it. In other words, the more passive managers of high-net-worth clients and the more active managers of low-net-worth clients were found to be the two groups worth targeting, a conclusion management understood and unhesitatingly accepted.

Can our segmentation register change?
Segmentations are viewed by too many of their sponsors as onetime, go-for-broke efforts to provide a comprehensive portrait of customers that can inform all subsequent marketing decisions. In our view, segmentations should be part of an ongoing search for answers to important business questions as they arise. Consequently, effective segmentations are dynamic—in two senses. First, they concentrate on consumers' needs, attitudes, and behavior, which can change quickly, rather than on personality traits, which usually endure throughout a person's life. Second, they are reshaped by market conditions, such as fluctuating economics, emerging consumer niches, and new technologies, which in today's world are evolving more rapidly than ever. In

short, effective segmentations focus on just one or two issues, and they need to be redrawn as soon as they have lost their relevance.

At the dawn of the World Wide Web, for example, a common segmentation criterion was the extent of a person's online experience. Early Adopters felt comfortable exploring the Web on their own; Newbies, or recent adopters, sought high levels of support. As newcomers became scarcer, the focus shifted to an emerging group of users, Transactors, for whom concern about sharing personal information, including credit card numbers, was no obstacle to transacting business online. Now that few people are worried about such things, many of today's segmentations tend to orient themselves around intrinsically Net-based services and functions such as games, parental control devices, and file sharing, each involving a set of separately measurable interests and concerns.

The Gravity of Decision Spectrum

The most common error marketers commit is applying segmentations designed to shed light on one kind of issue to some other purpose for which they were not designed. But which kinds of segmentations are best for which purposes? We suggest marketers begin by evaluating the expectations consumers bring to a particular kind of transaction. These can be located on our gravity of decision spectrum, which will tell you how deeply you need to probe consumers' motives, concerns, and even psyches.

Some decisions people make, such as trying a new brand of toilet paper or applying for a credit card, are relatively inconsequential. If the product is unsatisfactory, at worst a small amount of money has been wasted and a bit of inconvenience incurred. But decisions such as buying a home or choosing a cancer treatment have momentous significance given their potential for benefit or harm and the expense associated with them.

At the shallow end of the spectrum, consumers are seeking products and services they think will save them time, effort, and money. So segmentations for items such as toiletries and snacks try to measure things like the price sensitivity, habits, and impulsiveness of the target consumer. Segmentations for big-ticket purchases like cars and electronic devices, in the middle of the spectrum, test how

Effective segmentations focus on just one or two issues, and they need to be redrawn as soon as they have lost their relevance.

concerned consumers are about quality, design, complexity, and the status a product might confer. At the deepest end, consumers' emotional investment is great, and their core values are engaged. Those values are often in conflict with market values, and segmentations need to expose these tensions. Health care is the archetypal high-gravity issue. The exhibit, "What Is at Stake?" maps out the differences in business decisions, consumer decisions, and approaches to segmentation that emerge as the gravity of a consumer's buying decision increases.

What follows are three illustrations representing three points along the spectrum. Of course, many gradations exist between them.

The shallow end. A manufacturer of men's

shaving products faced a dilemma: how to spur fast growth when the firm already dominated the most profitable subcategory—shaving systems (a razor handle plus replaceable blades). Fearing it would cannibalize sales of its own shaving systems, the company shied away from disposable shavers, an obvious area to enter. But under pressure from senior management, the razor-and-blade business unit commissioned a new segmentation to find out whether there really was any basis for its fears.

Shavers are a small-ticket item. Though men naturally want to look neat and clean, most do not agonize over which technology or brand to choose, since all produce more or less the same result. Men's main concerns traditionally have been the comfort and closeness of the shave,

What Is at Stake?

Knowing how important a product or service is to your customers will help you decide which of their expectations are most likely to reveal their willingness to purchase your product. If your products are purely functional, you will probably want to investigate such garden-variety factors as the price sensitivity and brand loyalty of potential purchasers. But if such purchasers are facing life-altering choices, you will want to inquire into their most deeply held beliefs.

	Issues the business wants to address	Consumers' concerns	What the segmentation should try to find out
Shallowest decisions	• Whether to make small improvements to existing products • How to select targets of a media campaign • Whether to change prices	• How relevant and believable new-product claims are • How to evaluate a given product • Whether to switch products	• Buying and usage behavior • Willingness to pay a small premium for higher quality • Degree of brand loyalty
Middle-of-the-spectrum decisions	• How to position the brand • Which segments to pursue • Whether to change the product fundamentally • Whether to develop an entirely new product	• Whether to visit a clinic about a medical condition • Whether to switch one's brand of car • Whether to replace an enterprise software system	• Whether the consumers being studied are do-it-yourself or do-it-for-me types • Consumers' needs (better service, convenience, functionality) • Their social status, self-image, and lifestyle
Deepest decisions	• Whether to revise the business model in response to powerful social forces changing how people live their lives	• Choosing a course of medical treatment • Deciding where to live	• Core values and beliefs related to the buying decision

114

how easy the razor is to use (which often determines whether people favor a system or a disposable), and the price.

Accordingly, to determine whether a new product would cannibalize existing ones, a first segmentation used detailed household purchase records to put customers into one of three classifications: those who buy systems exclusively, those who buy disposables exclusively, and those who switch between the two. To management's surprise, the switching segment was very small, suggesting that the company could introduce a more expensive disposable razor without taking business away from its systems.

The next question was whether enough disposables users, who are thought of as looking for a low-cost way to shave, would buy a higher-quality but more expensive device. A second segmentation, therefore, sought to judge price sensitivity in order to reveal customers' propensity to trade up. As suspected, many men were not interested in a better disposable that cost more. However, the research did expose a modest level of emotional investment in the product on the part of young men who had girlfriends or were on the dating scene. For them, how their skin felt to the touch was almost as important as how they looked. Consequently, they would be willing to pay more for that smooth feel. Equipped with that insight, the company launched a very high-margin disposable, which garnered a solid and sustained market share without hurting its sister brands.

In the middle. In 1997, Toyota introduced a quirky internal combustion–electric hybrid vehicle to great success in its home market. But Americans were wary of the new technology. They sought greater power and faster acceleration at the Prius's price point. Moreover, in the late 1990s, U.S. drivers were mostly unconcerned about fuel consumption, an economic issue for some but not an environmental one.

Because even relatively inexpensive cars are large expenditures for most households and the cars people drive strongly influence their image in their own and others' eyes, some exploration of consumers' emotions and values was warranted. Accordingly, when Toyota did so, the carmaker discovered that about 10% of car buyers not only liked the car's design and accepted its performance but also were pleased

that it was less harmful to the environment than other cars. Although a Prius would be an adventurous purchase, in certain communities it might even be an admired one because of the values it represented. If the small group of potential purchasers could be reached efficiently rather than through an expensive media campaign, Toyota could make money on the car. As it turned out, the best prospects were contacted via the Internet, and the Prius easily met its first-year sales and profit targets.

The deep end. Continuing care retirement communities (CCRCs) are residential facilities for healthy and affluent retirees. Such a community typically includes single-family houses, duplexes, or flats where residents live before graduating into assisted-living or nursing care, both of which are available on the same campus. Sponsored by both nonprofit and for-profit institutions such as Hyatt, CCRCs have quintupled in number in the past 15 years.

CCRCs are expensive. Seniors pay a hefty entry fee—from \$125,000 to over \$400,000 (depending on the size and geographical location of the dwelling they choose) usually after selling the family home. Still, residents do not own their unit and thus do not build equity. A major component of the fee is an insurance policy that covers the cost of assisted living and skilled nursing care if the resident's health declines. Residents also pay a monthly fee covering meals, housekeeping, utilities, and other amenities. Even though a typical continuing care retirement community returns 90% of the initial fee when a resident moves out or dies, the individual or estate suffers a significant financial sacrifice, given the rate of appreciation of today's real estate market.

What, then, explains the demand for CCRCs? The answer was revealed by a segmentation oriented around changing family values. Published comments of CCRC residents and industry experts indicate that the segment of seniors attracted to this option is seeking to avoid dependence on family and longtime friends, who in earlier decades would have looked after them. Two key values characterize this segment:

• The desire for autonomy—to avoid being a burden on their loved ones;

• The willingness to embrace, in lieu of the security and warmth of having family and friends nearby, life in a quasi-institutional setting among strangers.

This segmentation obviously operates at the deepest level of the gravity of decision framework. It tells the retirement industry that adding Alzheimer's care to the package offered would appeal to the large numbers of the elderly who worry about becoming a burden and that proximity to or affiliation with a university would add to the sense of community valued in CCRCs.

• • •

Segmentation initiatives have generally been disappointing to the companies launching them. Their failures have mostly taken three forms. The first is excessive interest in consumers' identities, which has distracted marketers from the product features that matter most to current and potential customers of particular brands and categories. The second is too little emphasis on actual consumer behavior, which definitively reveals their attitudes and helps predict business outcomes. And the third is undue absorption in the technical details of devising segmentations, which estranges marketers from the decision makers on whose support their initiatives depend.

We believe that organizations able to overcome these three weaknesses will be able to respond more quickly and effectively to rapidly changing market conditions, develop insights into where and how to compete, and gain maximum benefit from scarce marketing resources. Nondemographic segmentation began more than 40 years ago as a way to focus on the differences among customers that matter the most strategically. Since for more than half of that span, it has not managed to do so, we hope that the rediscovery we are proposing here can make up for lost time and, over the next 40 years, at last fulfill segmentation's original purpose.

Reprint R0602G
To order, see the next page
or call 800-988-0886 or 617-783-7500
or go to www.hbr.org

Further Reading

The *Harvard Business Review* Paperback Series

Here are the landmark ideas—both contemporary and classic—that have established *Harvard Business Review* as required reading for businesspeople around the globe. Each paperback includes eight of the leading articles on a particular business topic. The series includes over thirty titles, including the following best-sellers:

Harvard Business Review on Brand Management
Product no. 1445

Harvard Business Review on Change
Product no. 8842

Harvard Business Review on Leadership
Product no. 8834

Harvard Business Review on Managing People
Product no. 9075

Harvard Business Review on Measuring Corporate Performance
Product no. 8826

For a complete list of the *Harvard Business Review* paperback series, go to www.hbr.org.

Harvard Business Review
www.hbr.org

U.S. and Canada
800-988-0886
617-783-7500
617-783-7555 fax

Focus Group Principles

Holly Edmunds

WHAT IS A FOCUS GROUP?

Focus groups are a form of qualitative research; a loosely structured means of obtaining opinions related to a specific topic. Groups usually consist of eight to ten people recruited and brought together based on pre-specified qualifications.

Focus groups are typically conducted in-person at a research facility, but more recently telefocus groups (via telephone conferencing) and Internet focus groups have become more popular. Generally two or more focus groups are conducted as part of a given study in order to provide comparisons between groups for greater detail in the research analysis.

WHEN TO USE FOCUS GROUPS

There are a wide variety of uses for focus groups. The most common uses are:

- Testing advertising copy or marketing promotions
- Positioning products or services
- Testing new concepts
- Testing usability of a product

Focus groups also can be used to generate ideas in a group brainstorming session. They are frequently utilized in developing questionnaires. By getting feedback in advance from people representative of those you hope to target with a survey, you can better word your questions and design clearer explanations of your concepts.

WHEN TO AVOID FOCUS GROUPS

While there are many instances where focus group research is helpful, there are equally as many situations where you should not use this methodology. Above all, it is important to remember that focus groups should not be used to make a final decision.

Results of focus groups are not statistically valid and should be used more as a thermometer to test the temperature of the market rather than as a ruler to provide precise measurements.

Likewise, the following represent good examples of when to avoid using focus groups:

- When you need a numerical response to questions like "what percentage . . . ?" or "how many . . . ?"
  Focus groups do not provide quantitative results.

- When you need to explore issues that are very personal or sensitive in nature.
  People are not really comfortable discussing personal topics in a group situation.

- When you want to set prices for your products or your services.
  Again, these results are not quantitative in nature hence it is not advisable to make final pricing decisions based on small group responses.

- When you cannot afford a survey.
  Focus groups are not a replacement for a survey. If what you really need are statistically valid results, consider a shorter survey or slightly reduced sample size, but do not rely on qualitative to give you the detail you require.

- When you want to validate internal decisions that cannot (or will not) be changed based on the results of the focus groups.
  If you will not be able to incorporate the results of the focus groups into product development, advertising design, etc., then there is no sense in conducting the groups in the first place.

Finally, before you opt to conduct focus groups, be certain that your audience (those people who will review and use the results of the study) are completely familiar with the type of results focus groups produce. If they expect to receive detailed graphs and tables, it may be very difficult to explain how to use qualitative data that will seem more vague in comparison.

LEAVE THE FOCUS GROUP TO THE PROFESSIONALS

At first glance, it seems quite simple to recruit people, gather them in a room and get the conversation rolling. While this may be less costly, if the groups are not conducted correctly there may ultimately be costs involved with incorrect interpretation of the discussion.

Secondly, a professional moderator runs a focus group. The moderator's job is directing the conversation and ensuring that all respondents voice their opinion. Experienced moderators spent years honing their skills – a charming conversationalist is no substitute for a professional.

Furthermore, consider the bias involved with moderating your own focus groups. How will you react in a focus group situation if the participants don't like the concepts? Will you probe for more details on their concerns or will you either (a) try to sell them on the concepts, (b) defend the concepts or (c) quickly try to steer them on to the next topic?

Using an outside vendor will provide the necessary element of objectivity into your study. Certainly, your views will be addressed in the groups, but the moderator is not as emotionally attached to your advertisements, products, etc., as someone internally is likely to be!

SETTING RESEARCH OBJECTIVES

There are specific steps involved in setting up any focus group study, beginning with determining your research objectives. Only the client can determine the objectives since that client is the one ultimately using the data. If objectives are not clearly defined, then the research vendor cannot be expected to answer the questions properly through the focus group process.

Research objectives should meet the following criteria:

- Objectives should be reviewed to determine that a qualitative methodology such as focus groups is the best means of getting the answers you require.

- Be specific with your stated objectives; vague questions cannot produce actionable solutions.

- If you have more than one objective, they should all be clearly related. Do not try to test a new product and a proposed advertising campaign in the same focus group. The group participants will become confused and the results will then become diluted.

DEFINING TARGET RECRUITS

You will also be expected as the client to provide inputs regarding the sampling process for your focus group study. Who do you need to talk to? These people will comprise your research sample. Again, it is imperative that you be very clear in your definitions.

Do your focus group participants need to currently use your product and/or your competitor's product?

- Should you be investigating the opinions of men or women or both?
- What about age ranges?
- And what about their television viewing habits?
- What industry should they work in?
- What positions should they hold?
- What is their total household income category?

These are just some examples of screening questions that will be asked by the vendor's interviewers during the focus group recruiting process.

Do you already have lists available of your customers? The vendor might be able to use these contacts in the recruiting process, thereby significantly reducing your recruiting expenses.

DESIGNING THE DISCUSSION GUIDE

The discussion guide is the outline that will be used by the focus group moderator in conducting the research conversation. Clients must be closely involved in designing the discussion guide to ensure that the focus group provides needed data.

There is one final note regarding your responsibilities as a client in a focus group study. Typically, your vendor will expect you to provide the final approval on both the screening questionnaire(s) for recruiting participants as well as focus group discussion guides.

If you still have questions or concerns at this point in the study, be sure to voice them. Do not let the study proceed unless you buy into the process, otherwise, doubts will remain when the final results are presented.

One caution, however. Let the moderator design the phrasing of each question. The client's job is to make sure all the relevant questions get answered. If you're taking the trouble to hire professionals to get those answers, don't try to micromanage the process.

The moderator has to keep the discussion going and ensure that it covers all of the topics in the discussion guide.

A good moderator encourages everyone to respond, prevents extremely vocal participants from taking over the conversation and prompts the shy ones to offer their opinions.

A moderator must understand the concepts being discussed, but not provide too much information. It is better to listen than to talk a lot since it is what the participants think that is really important.

Typically, the moderator will conduct or be involved in the debriefing sessions with the client.

The research vendor coordinates the focus group process as well as ensuring that the research is properly conducted.

The following are the specific tasks that the research vendor is typically responsible for:

- Development of the screening questionnaire(s).
- Recommendation of the sampling plan (and usually for obtaining lists of potential recruits).
- Design of the moderator's discussion guide.
- Arranging focus group facilities (including the host(ess), refreshments, and video and audiotaping).
- Obtaining co-op fees (cash incentives paid to participants for cooperating with the focus group process).
- Recruiting focus group participants (generally by telephone).
- Moderation of the focus groups.
- Debriefing sessions with the clients following each focus group or series of focus groups.
- Analysis and presentation of focus group results

CHOOSING A VENDOR

Check prior references for focus group research vendors before you consider having them conduct a study for you.

Consider the following issues:

- What experience does their moderator have?
- Is the vendor familiar with your industry?
- How well have they interpreted your needs in their proposal for the project?
- What is their timeline and does it meet your decision-making schedule?
- Are their costs in line with other vendors? If not, can they explain the differences?

So far, we have discussed focus groups in their most simplified form. Frequently, however, special situations do arise.

- International focus groups
- Research with children
- Studies involving elderly participants

Each of these situations involves some additional planning and considerations.

INTERNATIONAL FOCUS GROUPS

Focus group studies that include groups in foreign locations require special attention in a number of areas.

For example, the recruiting process may vary. In Germany, you cannot obtain the surname of participants or the precise names of the companies they work for given the stricter privacy laws. In Asian countries, recruiting may be more difficult by phone. Lists for countries outside of the U.S. may also be more difficult to obtain and may be more outdated.

Scheduling foreign groups requires an awareness of local customs and holidays. Focus groups in Europe tend to start later in the evening than those in the U.S. If you schedule groups in India on a religious holiday, your participation rate is likely to be low if anyone bothers to attend at all. Bear in mind the adage "when in Rome. . . ."

Facilities are frequently different in international locations. In the U.S., clients generally view groups from behind a one-way mirror. In other countries, viewing may be available only via a video monitor. In some instances, the video quality may not be what you would expect.

Translation is a major concern in foreign focus groups. All questionnaires must be properly translated and recruiting conducted in the local language. All materials to be used during the groups (i.e. advertisements, instruction sheets, etc.) must also be translated. The moderator must also be fluent in the language and interpretation (usually simultaneous) must be provided for the clients viewing the groups.

RESEARCH WITH CHILDREN

When recruiting children or teens for focus groups, first obtain permission from the parents to conduct the interview.

Keeping children's attention during a focus group is a challenge. Conference room chairs with wheels provide a distraction and the one-way mirror is an invitation to make some unique faces.

"Group-think" is more common in children's groups as well. Try to keep the groups in close age ranges and try not to let everyone in the group agree with the first child to offer an opinion.

Price-related questions or questions related to the past or future are more difficult for children to answer. It is better for questions to be worded in the present tense.

STUDIES INVOLVING ELDERLY PARTICIPANTS

Recruiting elderly people to participate in focus groups is frequently more difficult than recruiting other targets.

Unfortunately, the elderly are often the targets of marketing scams via telephone. As a result, they may be more cautious about being contacted to answer somewhat personal questions and attend a group. It is important to stress the legitimacy of the process and provide them with a number to call to confirm the existence of the research company.

Logistically, focus groups with seniors can be more difficult too. For example, many senior citizens no longer are able to drive. They will require public transportation or someone will have to bring them to the facility. This means your vendor should provide a waiting area for these additional people (but not invite them into the group). Likewise, the research facility should accommodate the elderly and handicapped with elevators, proper lighting, and safe parking.

Moderators should remember to speak clearly and somewhat louder than usual to ensure that all participants can hear the questions. Repetition of other participants' comments by the moderator can also be helpful. Concept materials for this age group should be easy to read.

As noted earlier, focus group evaluations are qualitative in nature and therefore do not include statistical data. Videotapes of each of the groups in the study are carefully reviewed and overall conclusions drawn. These tapes are particularly useful because they allow the researcher to see non-verbal reactions to concepts, advertisements, etc. Frequently transcripts of the groups are available for review to make it easier for the researcher to identify pertinent quotations.

The moderator often takes notes during the groups or writes responses on boards. These notations are also helpful in analysing focus group results. Occasionally, respondents complete brief questionnaires in the groups. This input, while not quantifiable, can provide help the researcher better understand the participants' responses and reactions.

Group similar responses by various qualifiers such as men versus women, company size, or geographic region. Frequently mentioned comments are considered relevant. Comments where participants appear to have been led by the moderator or other respondents should not be given much weight in the context of the evaluation.

Finally, always remember that the results of a focus group study provide a general direction or test of the market, not a statistical evaluation.

SERVQUAL and Model of Service Quality Gaps:
A Framework for Determining and Prioritizing Critical Factors in Delivering Quality Services

Dr. Arash Shahin

Department of Management, University of Isfahan, Iran

E–Mail: *arashshahin@hotmail.com*

Abstract

Service firms like other organizations are realizing the significance of customer–centered philosophies and are turning to quality management approaches to help managing their businesses. This paper has started with the concept of service quality and has demonstrated the model of service quality gaps. SERVQUAL as an effective approach has been studied and its role in the analysis of the difference between customer expectations and perceptions has been highlighted with support of an example. Outcomes of the study outline the fact that although SERQUAL could close one of the important service quality gaps associated with external customer services, it could be extended to close other major gaps and therefore, it could be developed in order to be applied for internal customers, i.e. employees and service providers.

Key words: *Service, Quality, Gaps, SERVQUAL, Customer, Expectations, Perceptions*

INTRODUCTION

Managers in the service sector are under increasing pressure to demonstrate that their services are customer–focused and that continuous performance improvement is being delivered. Given the financial and resource constraints under which service organisations must manage it is essential that customer expectations are properly understood and measured and that, from the customers' perspective, any gaps in service quality are identified. This information then assists a manager in identifying cost–effective ways of closing service quality gaps and of prioritizing which gaps to focus on—a critical decision given scarce resources.

While there have been efforts to study service quality, there has been no general agreement on the measurement of the concept. The majority of the work to date has attempted to use the SERVQUAL (Parasuraman *et al.,* 1985; 1988) methodology in an effort to measure service quality (e.g. Brooks *et al.,* 1999; Chaston, 1994; Edvardsson *et al.,* 1997; Lings and Brooks, 1998; Reynoso and Moore, 1995; Young and Varble, 1997; Sahney *et al.,* 2004).

One of the aims of this study involves the use of SERVQUAL instrument in order to ascertain any actual or perceived gaps between customer expectations and perceptions of the service offered. Another aim of this paper is to point out how management of service improvement can become more logical and integrated with respect to the prioritized service quality dimensions and their affections on increasing/decreasing service quality gaps. In the following, after a brief review of the service quality concept, the model of service quality gaps and the SERVQUAL methodology is demonstrated and an example is presented to pinpoint the application of the SERVQUAL approach. Then, after a discussion, major conclusions are derived.

SERVICE QUALITY

Service quality is a concept that has aroused considerable interest and debate in the research literature because of the difficulties in both defining it and measuring it with no overall consensus emerging on either (Wisniewski, 2001). There are a number of different "definitions" as to what is meant by service quality. One that is commonly used defines service quality as the extent to which a service meets customers' needs or expectations (Lewis and Mitchell, 1990; Dotchin and Oakland, 1994a; Asubonteng *et al.,* 1996; Wisniewski and Donnelly, 1996). Service quality can thus be defined as the difference between customer expectations of service and perceived service. If expectations are greater than performance, then perceived quality is less than satisfactory and hence customer dissatisfaction occurs (Parasuraman *et al.,* 1985; Lewis and Mitchell, 1990).

Always there exists an important question: why should service quality be measured? Measurement allows for comparison before and after changes, for the location of quality related problems and for the establishment of clear standards for service delivery. Edvardsen *et al.* (1994) state that, in their experience, the starting point in developing quality in services is analysis and measurement. The SERVQUAL approach, which is studied in this paper is the most common method for measuring service quality.

MODEL OF SERVICE QUALITY GAPS

There are seven major gaps in the service quality concept, which are shown in Figure 1. The model is an extention of Parasuraman *et al.* (1985). According to the following explanation (ASI Quality Systems, 1992; Curry, 1999; Luk and Layton, 2002), the three important gaps, which are more associated with the external customers are Gap1, Gap5 and Gap6; since they have a direct relationship with customers.

- **Gap1: Customers' expectations versus management perceptions:** as a result of the lack of a marketing research orientation, inadequate upward communication and too many layers of management.

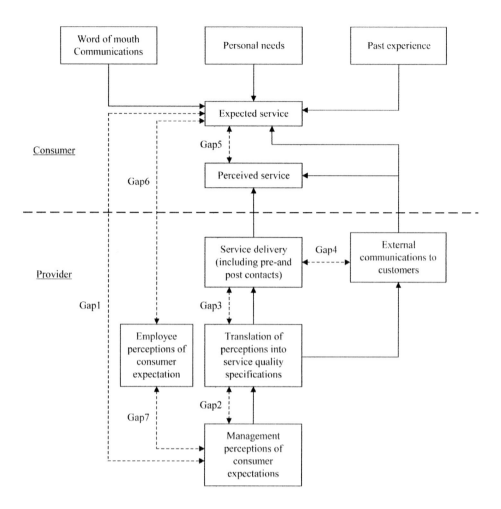

- **Gap2: Management perceptions versus service specifications:** as a result of inadequate commitment to service quality, a perception of unfeasibility, inadequate task standardisation and an absence of goal setting.

- **Gap3: Service specifications versus service delivery:** as a result of role ambiguity and conflict, poor employee-job fit and poor technology-job fit, inappropriate supervisory control systems, lack of perceived control and lack of teamwork.

- **Gap4: Service delivery versus external communication:** as a result of inadequate horizontal communications and propensity to over-promise.

- **Gap5: The discrepancy between customer expectations** and their perceptions of the service delivered: as a result of the influences exerted from the customer side and the shortfalls (gaps) on the part of the service provider. In this case, customer expectations are influenced by the extent of personal needs, word of mouth recommendation and past service experiences.

- **Gap6: The discrepancy between customer expectations and employees' perceptions:** as a result of the differences in the understanding of customer expectations by front–line service providers.
- **Gap7: The discrepancy between employee's perceptions and management perceptions:** as a result of the differences in the understanding of customer expectations between managers and service providers.

According to Brown and Bond (1995), "the gap model is one of the best received and most heuristically valuable contributions to the services literature". The model identifies seven key discrepancies or gaps relating to managerial perceptions of service quality, and tasks associated with service delivery to customers. The first six gaps (Gap 1, Gap 2, Gap 3, Gap 4, Gap 6 and Gap 7) are identified as functions of the way in which service is delivered, whereas Gap 5 pertains to the customer and as such is considered to be the true measure of service quality. The Gap on which the SERVQUAL methodology has influence is Gap 5. In the following, the SERVQUAL approach is demonstrated.

SERVQUAL METHODOLOGY

Clearly, from a Best Value perspective the measurement of service quality in the service sector should take into account customer expectations of service as well as perceptions of service. However, as Robinson (1999) concludes: "It is apparent that there is little consensus of opinion and much disagreement about how to measure service quality". One service quality measurement model that has been extensively applied is the SERVQUAL model developed by Parasuraman *et al.* (1985, 1986, 1988, 1991, 1993, 1994; Zeithaml *et al.,* 1990). SERVQUAL as the most often used approach for measuring service quality has been to compare customers' expectations before a service encounter and their perceptions of the actual service delivered (Gronroos, 1982; Lewis and Booms, 1983; Parasuraman *et al.,* 1985). The SERVQUAL instrument has been the predominant method used to measure consumers' perceptions of service quality. It has five generic dimensions or factors and are stated as follows (van Iwaarden *et al.,* 2003):

(1) *Tangibles.* Physical facilities, equipment and appearance of personnel.
(2) *Reliability.* Ability to perform the promised service dependably and accurately.
(3) *Responsiveness.* Willingness to help customers and provide prompt service.
(4) *Assurance* (including competence, courtesy, credibility and security). Knowledge and courtesy of employees and their ability to inspire trust and confidence.
(5) *Empathy* (including access, communication, understanding the customer). Caring and individualized attention that the firm provides to its customers.

In the SERVQUAL instrument, 22 statements (Appendix I) measure the performance across these five dimensions, using a seven point likert scale measuring both customer expectations and perceptions (Gabbie and O'neill, 1996). It is important to note that without adequate information on both the quality of services expected and perceptions of services received then feedback from customer surveys can be highly misleading from both a policy and an operational perspective.

In the following, the application of SERVQUAL approach is more specified with an example in a catering company.

Example

In an investigation conducted by Bryslan and Curry (2001) in a catering company, a total of 140 questionnaires were distributed to all of the previous year's customers and 52 useable questionnaires were returned, resulting in a 37 per cent response rate. As can be seen from Table I, all questionnaire responses were negative and an overall departmental weighted SERVQUAL score of –1.6 was recorded, indicating a significant shortfall in meeting customer expectations across all service areas and dimensions. The summary scores for each dimension are shown in Table I, with the weighted average scores per dimension having been totalled to achieve the overall SERVQUAL score. As can be seen from Table I, the highest gap scores were for Reliability and Responsiveness; this is real cause for concern and provides a definite staring point for service improvements. As can be seen from the results, the customer expects most from the Reliability dimension of the catering service. The relatively low importance of Tangibles could be attributable to the fact that customers are aware of the financial constraints which are typical in the local authority funding context, and simply do not expect much when it comes to aesthetics; instead, they attach more importance to the delivery aspects of the service. Customers allocated to Assurance the lowest weighting, indicating it to be of least importance to them, yet they expect most from this service dimension. This apparent anomaly is probably due to the fact that customers expect staff to be knowledgeable about the service and therefore they can see no reason for this dimension not to be achieved. It is assumed that for this reason, customers have weighted this dimension lowest.

Discussion

The research on measuring service quality has focused primarily on how to meet or exceed the external customer's expectations, and has viewed service quality as a measure of how the delivered service level matches consumer's expectations. These perspectives can also be applied to the employees of a firm and in this case, other major gaps could be closed in the service quality gaps model (Kang *et al.*, 2002).

The concept of measuring the difference between expectations and perceptions in the form of the SERVQUAL gap score proved very useful for assessing levels of service quality. Parasuraman *et al.*, argue that, with minor modification, SERVQUAL can be adapted to any service organisation. They further argue that information on service quality gaps can help managers diagnose where performance improvement can best be targeted. The largest negative gaps, combined with assessment of where expectations

TABLE 1   SERVQUAL Scores for Catering Services (Bryslan and Curry, 2001)

Dimension	Expectations	Perceptions	Gap scores	Weightings	Weighted Average
Tangibles	5.66	4.26	–1.40	19.8	–0.28
Reliability	6.06	4.36	–1.70	29.6	–0.5
Responsiveness	5.74	4.05	–1.69	19.9	–0.34
Assurance	6.13	4.58	–1.55	15.2	–0.24
Empathy	5.97	4.45	–1.52	15.7	–0.24

Note: Overall average weighted SERVQUAL score = –1.6

are highest, facilitates prioritisation of performance improvement. Equally, if gap scores in some aspects of service do turn out to be positive, implying expectations are actually not just being met but exceeded, then this allows managers to review whether they may be "over-supplying" this particular feature of the service and whether there is potential for re-deployment of resources into features which are underperforming.

It seems that in almost all the existing resources, the SERVQUAL approach has been used only for closing Gap 5. However, its application could also be extended to the analysis of other gaps. It is important to note that SERVQUAL is only one of the instruments used in service quality analysis and there are different approaches which might be stronger in closing gaps. SERVQUAL has been extensively criticised on both theoretical and operational grounds (see Buttle, 1996 and Asubonteng *et al.*, 1996), although Asubonteng *et al.* (1996) conclude that: "Until a better but equally simple model emerges, SERVQUAL will predominate as a service quality measure". It is also evident that SERVQUAL by itself, useful though it may be to a service manager, will not give a complete picture of needs, expectations and perceptions in a service organization context. As Gaster (1995) comments, "because service provision is complex, it is not simply a matter of meeting expressed needs, but of finding out unexpressed needs, setting priorities, allocating resources and publicly justifying and accounting for what has been done". Service organizations are responsible and accountable to citizens and communities as well as to customers and service users. There are wider service organization agendas than simply service quality: improving access to existing services; equity and equality of service provision; providing efficient and effective services within political as well as resource constraints. The definition of service quality therefore takes on a wider meaning and accordingly its measurement becomes both more complex and more difficult.

Besides the discussed weaknesses, a particular advantage of SERVQUAL is that it is a tried and tested instrument which can be used comparatively for benchmarking purposes (Brysland and Curry, 2001). SERVQUAL does, however, benefit from being a statistically valid instrument as a result of extensive field testing and refinement. It therefore escapes the pitfall of being perceived by service users and providers as "something that has been invented off the top of the head" or a questionnaire that has been skewed to elicit certain types of response. As a generic and universally-applicable instrument, SERVQUAL can also be administered on a repeated, regular basis and used for comparative benchmarking purposes. To appreciate more fully the benefits of using SERVQUAL, surveys should be conducted every year, for the following reasons:

- to allow yearly comparisons;
- to determine how service improvements have affected customers' perceptions and expectations of the service over time; and
- to determine the effectiveness of service development and improvement initiatives in targeted dimensions.

It is important to note that the measurement systems themselves are often inappropriate because the system designers do not know enough about what is to be measured. Measuring customer perceptions of service may increase expectations and measuring too often may well result in customers losing their motivation to answer correctly. Finally, there is no point in measuring service quality if one is not willing to take appropriate action on the findings.

Conclusions

In this paper, service quality and its model of gaps were reviewed. SERVQUAL methodology as an analytical approach for evaluating the difference between customers' expectations and perceptions of quality was also studied.

While this research provides some perspectives to the field of service quality, it is believed that there are a number of things that should be done to confirm the demonstrated methodologies as well as to expand the use of SERVQUAL in design and improvement of quality services.

Just as the SERVQUAL instrument is extensively used to assess external service quality, the instrument can also be modified to assess the quality of the internal service provided by departments and divisions within a company to employees in other departments and divisions. The results of the current study illustrate that organizations can at least assess five dimensions of service quality to ascertain the level of services provided, and to determine which dimensions need improvement.

In order to improve service quality, it is necessary to contact employees regularly and assess their service experiences. Like the external customer, an internal customer too considers categories of service attributes, such as reliability and responsiveness, in judging the quality of the internal service. With the knowledge of the internal service quality dimensions, the service organizations can then judge how well the organization or employees performed on each dimension and managers could identify the weakness in order to make improvements.

Future research should seek to examine the use of SERVQUAL to close other service quality gaps for different types of organizations. Also, an important issue for future research is about the relationship between internal service quality and external customer satisfaction as well as other constructs, such as employee service orientation, and external service quality.

In conclusion, knowing how customers perceive the service quality and being able to measure service quality can benefit industry professionals in quantitative and qualitative ways. The measurement of service quality can provide specific data that can be used in quality management; hence, service organizations would be able to monitor and maintain quality service. Assessing service quality and better understanding how various dimensions affect overall service quality would enable organizations to efficiently design the service delivery process. By identifying strengths and weaknesses pertaining to the dimensions of service quality organizations can better allocate resources to provide better service and ultimately better service to external customers.

Generally speaking, the study of service quality is both important and challenging. Future efforts should continue to advance the understanding of the concept and the means to measure and improve service quality.

REFERENCE

ASI Quality Systems (1992), *Quality function deployment—Practitioner workshop,* American Supplier Institute Inc., USA.

Asubonteng, P., McCleary, K.J. and Swan, J.E. (1996), "SERVQUAL revisited: a critical review of service quality", *Journal of Services Marketing,* Vol. 10, No. 6, pp. 62–81.

Brooks, R.F., Lings, I.N. and Botschen, M.A. (1999), "Internal marketing and customer driven wavefronts", *Service Industries Journal,* Vol. 19, No. 4, pp. 49–67.

Brown, S.W. and Bond, E.U. III (1995), "The internal/external framework and service quality: Toward theory in services marketing", *Journal of Marketing Management,* February, pp. 25–39.

Brysland, A. and Curry, A. (2001), "Service improvements in public services using SERVQUAL", *Managing Service Quality,* Vol. 11, No. 6, pp. 389–401.

Chaston, I. (1994), "Internal customer management and service gaps within the UK manufacturing sector", *International Journal of Operations and Production,* Vol. 14, No. 9, pp. 45–56.

Curry, A. (1999), "Innovation in public service management", *Managing Service Quality,* Vol. 9, No. 3, pp. 180–190.

Dotchin, J.A. and Oakland, J.S. (1994a), "Total quality management in services: Part 2 Service quality", *International Journal of Quality & Reliability Management,* Vol. 11, No. 3, pp. 27–42.

Edvardsen, B., Tomasson, B. and Ovretveit, J. (1994), *Quality of Service: Making it Really Work,* McGraw-Hill, New York, NY.

Edvardsson, B., Larsson, G. and Setterlind, S. (1997), "Internal service quality and the psychological work environment: an empirical analysis of conceptual interrelatedness", *Service Industries Journal,* Vol. 17, No. 2, pp. 252–63.

Gabbie, O. and O'Neill, M.A. (1996) SERVQUAL and the northern Ireland hotel sector: A comparative analysis—Part 1, *Managing Service Quality,* Vol. 6, No. 6, pp. 25–32.

Gaster, L. (1995), *Quality in Public Services,* Open University Press, Buckingham.

Gronroos, C. (1982), *Strategic Management and Marketing in the Service Sector,* Swedish School of Economics and Business Administration, Helsingfors.

Kang, G.D., James, J., and Alexandris, K. (2002) Measurement of internal service quality: Application of the SERVQUAL battery to internal service quality, *Managing Service Quality,* Vol. 12, No. 5, pp. 278–291.

Lewis, B.R. and Mitchell, V.W. (1990), "Defining and measuring the quality of customer service", *Marketing Intelligence & Planning,* Vol. 8, No. 6, pp. 11–17.

Lewis, R.C. and Booms, B.H. (1983), "The marketing aspects of service quality", in Berry, L., Shostack, G. and Upah, G. (Eds), Emerging Perspectives on Services Marketing, American Marketing Association, Chicago, IL, pp. 99–107.

Lings, I.N. and Brooks, R.F. (1998), "Implementing and measuring the effectiveness of internal marketing", *Journal of Marketing Management,* Vol. 14, pp. 325–51.

Luk, Sh.T.K. and Layton, R. (2002), "Perception Gaps in customer expectations: Managers versus service providers and customers", *The Service Industries Journal,* Vol. 22, No. 2, April, pp. 109–128.

Reynoso, J. and Moore, B. (1995), "Towards the measurement of internal service quality", *International Journal of Service Industry Management,* Vol. 6, No. 3, pp. 64–83.

Parasuraman, A., Zeithaml, V.A. and Berry, L.L. (1985), "A conceptual model of service quality and its implication", *Journal of Marketing,* Vol. 49, Fall, pp. 41–50.

Parasuraman, A., Zeithaml, V.A. and Berry, L.L. (1986), "SERVQUAL: a multiple–item scale for measuring customer perceptions of service quality", *Report No. 86–108,* Marketing Science Institute, Cambridge, MA.

Parasuraman, A., Zeithaml, V.A. and Berry, L.L. (1988), "SERVQUAL: a multi-item scale for measuring consumer perceptions of the service quality", *Journal of Retailing,* Vol. 64, No. 1, pp. 12–40.

Parasuraman, A., Zeithaml, V.A. and Berry, L.L. (1991), "Refinement and reassessment of the SERVQUAL scale", *Journal of Retailing,* Vol. 67, pp. 420–450.

Parasuraman, A., Zeithaml, V.A. and Berry, L.L. (1993), "Research note: more on improving service quality measurement", *Journal of Retailing*, Vol. 69, No. 1, pp. 140–147.

Parasuraman, A., Zeithaml, V.A. and Berry, L.L. (1994), "Reassessment of expectations as a comparison standard in measuring service quality: implications for future research", *Journal of Marketing*, Vol. 58, pp. 111–124.

Robinson, S. (1999), "Measuring service quality: current thinking and future requirements", *Marketing Intelligence & Planning*, Vol. 17, No. 1, pp. 21–32.

Sahney, S., Banwet, D.K., and Karunes, S. (2004), "A SERVQUAL and QFD approach to total quality education: A student perspective", *International Journal of Productivity and Performance Management*, Vol. 53, No. 2, pp. 143–166.

Van Iwaarden, J., van der Wiele, T., Ball, L., and Millen, R. (2003), "Applying SERVQUAL to web sites: An exploratory study", *International Journal of Quality & Reliability Management*, Vol.20, No.8, pp. 919–935.

Wisniewski, M. (2001), "Using SERVQUAL to assess customer satisfaction with public sector services", *Managing Service Quality*, Vol. 11, No. 6, pp. 380–388.

Wisniewski, M. and Donnelly, M. (1996), "Measuring service quality in the public sector: the potential for SERVQUAL", *Total Quality Management*, Vol. 7, No. 4, pp. 357–365.

Zeithaml, V.A., Parasuraman, A. and Berry, L.L. (1990), Delivering quality service; Balancing customer perceptions and expectations, *The Free Press*, New York, NY.

APPENDIX I
22 Statements of the SERVQUAL Instrument

DIRECTIONS: This survey deals with your opinions of——— services. Please show the extent to which you think firms offering ——— services should possess the features described by each statement. Do this by picking one of the seven numbers next to each statement. If you strongly agree that these firms should possess a feature, circle the number 7. If you strongly disagree that these firms should possess a feature, circle 1. If your feelings are not strong, circle one of the numbers in the middle. There are no right or wrong answers. All we are interested in is a number that best shows your expectations about firms offering ——— services.

E1. They should have up–to–date equipment.
E2. Their physical facilities should be visually appealing.
E3. Their employees should be well dressed and appear neat.
E4. The appearance of the physical facilities of these firms should be in keeping with the type of services provided.
E5. When these firms promise to do something by a certain time, they should do so.
E6. When customers have problems, these firms should be sympathetic and reassuring.
E7. These firms should be dependable.
E8. They should provide their services at the time they promise to do so.
E9. They should keep their records accurately.
E10. They shouldn't be expected to tell customers exactly when services will be performed. (–)
E11. It is not realistic for customers to expect prompt service from employees of these firms. (–)
E12. Their employees don't always have to be willing to help customers. (–)
E13. It is okay if they are too busy to respond to customer requests promptly. (–)
E14. Customers should be able to trust employees of these firms.

E15. Customers should be able to feel safe in their transactions with these firms' employees.

E16. Their employees should be polite.

E17. Their employees should get adequate support from these firms to do their jobs well.

E18. These firms should not be expected to give customers individual attention. (–)

E19. Employees of these firms cannot be expected to give customers personal attention. (–)

E20. It is unrealistic to expect employees to know what the needs of their customers are. (–)

E21. It is unrealistic to expect these firms to have their customers' best interests at heart. (–)

E22. They shouldn't be expected to have operating hours convenient to all their customers. (–)

DIRECTIONS: The following set of statements relate to your feelings about XYZ. For each statement, please show the extent to which you believe XYZ has the feature described by the statement. Once again, circling a 7 means that you strongly agree that XYZ has that feature, and circling a 1 means that you strongly disagree. You may circle any of the numbers in the middle that show how strong your feelings are. There are no right or wrong answers. All we are interested in is a number that best shows your perceptions about XYZ.

P1. XYZ has up–to–date equipment.

P2. XYZ's physical facilities are visually appealing.

P3. XYZ's employees are well dressed and appear neat.

P4. The appearance of the physical facilities of XYZ is in keeping with the type of services provided.

P5. When XYZ promises to do something by a certain time, it does so.

P6. When you have problems, XYZ is sympathetic and reassuring.

P7. XYZ is dependable.

P8. XYZ provides its services at the time it promises to do so.

P9. XYZ keeps its records accurately.

P10. XYZ does not tell customers exactly when services will be performed. (–)

P11. You do not receive prompt service from XYZ's employees. (–)

P12. Employees of XYZ are not always willing to help customers. (–)

P13. Employees of XYZ are too busy to respond to customer requests promptly. (–)

P14. You can trust employees of XYZ.

P15. You feel safe in your transactions with XYZ's employees.

P16. Employees of XYZ arc polite.

P17. Employees get adequate support from XYZ to do their jobs well.

P18. XYZ does not give you individual attention. (–)

P19. Employees of XYZ do not give you personal attention. (–)

P20. Employees of XYZ do not know what your needs are. (–)

P21. XYZ does not have your best interests at heart. (–)

P22. XYZ does not have operating hours convenient to all their customers. (–)